Clear
Your
Desk!

Clear Your Desk!

**The Definitive Guide to
Conquering Your Paper
Workload – Forever!**

Declan Treacy

Upstart Publishing Company, Inc.
The Small Business Publishing Company
Dover, New Hampshire

Published by Upstart Publishing Company, Inc.
A Division of Dearborn Publishing Group, Inc.
12 Portland Street
Dover, New Hampshire 03820
(800) 235-8866 or (603) 749-5071

First published by Business Books Limited
An imprint of Random Century Limited
20 Vauxhall Bridge Road
London SW1V 2SA

Neither the author nor the publisher of this book is engaged in
rendering, by the sale of this book, legal, accounting, or other
professional services. The reader is encouraged to employ the services of
a competent professional in such matters.

Library of Congress Cataloging-in-Publication Data
Treacy, Declan.
    Clear your desk! : the definitive guide to conquering your paper
workload—forever! / Declan Treacy.
    p.   cm.
    Includes index.
    ISBN 0-936894-38-5 : $14.95
    1. Paperwork (Office practice: I. Title.
HF5547.15.T73   1992
651.5—dc20   92-30260
                                                                  CIP

Printed in the United States of America
10 9 8 7 6 5 4 3 2 1

Cover design by Pear Graphic Design, Portsmouth, N.H.

For a complete catalog of Upstart's small business publications call, (800)
235-8866.

Contents

Forward vii

1. THE PAPERWORK JUNGLE 1

The paperless office – Paperwork costs – To clear or not to clear? – The myths surrounding the cluttered desk – What is your current backlog of paperwork?

2. PAPERWORK PROBLEMS 21

Executives who work at cluttered desks work longer hours – A cluttered desk means you will get less done – A cluttered desk is a breeding ground for crises – Distractions, distractions, distractions – Losing things – Ending up doing the work of others – Procrastination leads to clutter leads to procrastination – Stress and the cluttered desk

3. ELIMINATING UNNECESSARY PAPERWORK 43

Reducing unnecessary reports – Stamping out standard forms – Eliminating unnecessary memos – Eliminating unnecessary procedures – How to reduce the time you spend on other people's paperwork – Coping with a paperholic boss – Reducing the inflow of paperwork from outside the organization. Eliminating self-generated chaos

4. PAPERWORK: THE FOUR CHOICES 85

Deal with each piece of paper as soon as it lands on the desk! – Make one of four choices about each piece of paper – Paperwork diary: the Act on, Pass on, File, Discard process in action

5. PRIORITY PAPERWORK 103
$25,000 advice - Defining your ownpriorities

6. CLEAR YOUR FILING SYSTEM! 127
The hoarding habit - Filing disorder - The two approaches
to filing

7. CLEAR YOUR DESK! - ACTION PLAN 149
Organizing an in-company *Clear Your Desk!* day

Index 163

Foreword

International Clear Your Desk! Day was launched in 1990 as a day when office workers around the world would stop work to clear the clutter from their desks. The day is co-ordinated by The Clear Your Desk! Organization and in 1991 fell on Friday, 26 April. The enthusiastic participation in this event has prompted the writing of this book. The struggle against unnecessary paperwork is universal and whether or not you work from a cluttered desk you will recognize many of the problems discussed here.

The book is dedicated to all those people who have attended the Clear Your Desk! seminar and who have successfully organized in-company Clear Your Desk! days. I am also grateful to Sir John Harvey-Jones, Gerald Ratner, Anita Roddick, Richard Branson, Sir Allen Sheppard, and Professor George Bain for their thought-provoking contributions.

Declan Treacy
The Clear Your Desk! Organization
27 Old Gloucester Street
London WC1N 3XX
Tel: 081 903 7261

CHAPTER ONE

The Paperwork Jungle

Less paper is good, zero paper is best .... People creating, handling and moving large volumes of paper are almost certainly not being employed to best advantage. In small doses paper often appears inexpensive, cost effective, easy to use, not requiring capital investment and it is familiar. In large volumes, however, paper processing is the bane of any service organization.

—Michael P. Zampino
Citibank Corporation

THE WAR AGAINST unnecessary paperwork is on. The mission is two fold: to help individuals cope more effectively with their paper workloads and to reduce the level of bureaucratic paperwork in organizations throughout the world. The battle cry is *Clear Your Desk!* The starting point is now.

Since the first piece of paper was produced in A.D. 105 by Tsai Luin, the Chinese Minister of Agriculture, its use has grown alarmingly. Nearly 2,000 years later paper has become the foundation on which our organizations are built. There hardly seems to be a business operation or communication system that does not involve paperwork. At the beginning of the 1990's office workers around the world used more than 15 million miles of paper every day. The smooth flow of paperwork, essential to an effectively functioning organization has become an uncontrolled avalanche. In the U.S. alone, businesses currently have over 300 billion pieces of paper on file, a hoard which is growing by more than 72 billion pages each year. As well as an organization's internal paperwork there is a massive inflow of paper from outside the organization. Over two billion business letters are posted around the world every day. The U.K. government issues nearly two billion forms every year, 36 for every man, woman and child in the country.

While a large proportion of this paperwork is important, we have reached a situation where most organizations, both public and private, are suffocating under mountains of unwanted paper.

Millions of working hours are wasted in processing paperwork which should never have been introduced in the first place. Everywhere we turn there are standard forms waiting to be completed, forms that are over-complicated and that ask for information already available elsewhere. There are many organizations, not just those that are traditionally seen as paper intensive, where decisions cannot be made without the production of voluminous reports to justify them. In addition, there are the bureaucratic procedures which place paperwork in the way of getting a job done and stifle all innovation. Customers' needs are ignored as common sense is replaced by bureaucracy.

Staff morale suffers seriously as a result of trying to cope with huge piles of paperwork. In the U.K. the Inland Revenue receives 155 million pieces of mail each year. In 1985 there was a backlog of 6.2 million pieces of paper awaiting attention. The situation has improved somewhat since then but there are still 2.7 million items waiting to be dealt with. The feeling that no matter how hard they work there will still be a backlog of paperwork is one which is familiar to many people.

The stream of paper flowing onto the desk is constant and looking around any organization will reveal stacks of unfinished paperwork mounting up on people's desks. Research has shown that the average office worker has a backlog of 40 hours of paperwork on the desk. Stacks of unfinished paperwork are made up of bulging files, Post-it™ notes, reports, faxes, letters, computer printouts, newsletters, brochures, pads, dia-ries, standard forms, reference books, memo pads, magazines and more ....Almost every activity we com-plete involves some paperwork. Office workers worldwide produce 32 pages of computer printout, make 18 photocopies, file away ten documents, retrieve and refile another five and originate more than four pages of reports and other documents *every single day*. European office workers hoard an average of more than 20,000 pieces of paper in their offices with a significant proportion of that on their desks. Every year an additional 5,000 pieces of paper join that stockpile with only 3,000 being discarded.

We spend at least 50 percent of our working lives struggling to get to grips with paperwork. The development of effective paper handling skills is, however, an area which has been completely ignored.

THE PAPERLESS OFFICE!

The belief that the paperless office is almost here is one of the main reasons why organizations have put so little effort into training their staff to cope more effectively with paperwork. Since the early 1970's the information technology gurus have been predicting the advent of the paperless office, an organizational nirvana where all information is transferred invisibly and at high speed through computer networks. We only have to look at our desktops to see that it has not yet arrived. The number of office workers with desktop computers is increasing all the time, yet those computers are invariably surrounded by mountains of paper. The statistics back up our initial observations. Computer printers produce over two and a half million pieces of paper every minute throughout the world. Sixty million pages are duplicated every hour by photocopiers and over 30 billion faxes are sent worldwide every year. Rather than freeing office workers from the paperwork burden, technology has actually increased it. Paper is here to stay, that is unless someone develops the paperless printer and the paperless photocopier.

The paperless office!

PAPERWORK COSTS

The costs associated with paperwork are a major drain on the profits of most organizations, although few studies have been completed to determine exactly what those costs are. However, U.K.-research has shown that on average, for every £1 spent on printing forms, £40 is spent on processing them. In the U.S. it has been estimated that the cost to the economy of government paperwork is in excess of $100 billion a year. A Canadian study found that its businesses were spending over $500 million a year on storing over 170 million cubic meters of paper.

There are two main types of cost associated with paperwork: paper costs and costs in terms of time and resources. Paper costs are negligible compared with the latter; paper costs about two cents per sheet—a sum which does not stretch organizational resources. People are currently more concerned with the cost to the environment of paper usage than what paper actually costs monetarily. About 25 million trees are cut down to meet the U.K.'s paper needs alone every year. While recycling office paper is a mild remedy for this situation, it would be far more beneficial to use less paper in the first place. It is far better to eliminate an unnecessary 100-page report which is sent to 20 people than it is to recycle the 2,000 pages after its use.

The costs in use of paper are where the real problems lie. The time wasted in organizations producing, distributing and reading unnecessary memos and reports is enormous. Organizational resources are also soaked up in processing standard forms which should never have been introduced. If the office workers in your company spend 50 percent of their time on paperwork, then assuming an average salary of $28,500 the paperwork cost per individual per annum is $14,000. One hundred office workers dealing with paperwork will cost $1,400,000 per annum in salaries and a large part of that will be unnecessary. There is also the cost of lost opportunities to the organization to be considered. Time spent dealing with paperwork is often time not spent doing the job. While one company's salespeople are pushing pieces of paper around desks, their competitors will be out in the marketplace meeting customers and making sales.

Individuals' lack of effective paper handling skills adds significantly to the costs of paperwork. The office worker with a cluttered desk will spend about 7 percent of his or her time trying to locate documents on the desktop. When you consider the cost of time spent by 100 office workers looking for pieces of paper over one year—$160,000—the statistics begin to look frightening. Respondents to the Clear Your Desk! survey★ admitted to spending more than five hours a week fire-fighting because of paperwork ineffectively dealt with the first time around. The cost of supporting your 100-strong group of office workers to manage their crises adds up to $372,000 per annum.

The potential for significant cost reduction and productivity gains is quite clear. The paperwork epidemic must be tackled on two fronts. The mountain of bureaucratic paperwork must be attacked from the top down and nothing short of ruthlessness will prove successful. The battle against piles of paper that build up unnecessarily on your desk can be fought and won only by yourself.

TO CLEAR OR NOT TO CLEAR?

The need to work from an uncluttered desk has long been stressed. In 1918, *The Optimum Book for Offices* warned against using desks as filing systems and recommended that executives had a specific place for different items, objects, files and papers. Over 70 years later we are still hoarding mountains of paper on our desks. The question often asked, "If most people work from cluttered desks why should they clear paper from the desktop and change the way they work?" can be answered with many good reasons why you should work from a clear desk.

If you have stacks of paper strewn across the desk then quite clearly you will spend more time trying to locate specific documents than if you had them neatly filed away. It is straightforward logic that if you hoard low pay-off paperwork on the desk rather than throwing it in the bin you are more likely to waste time working

★ Conducted in 1990. 1,000 office workers in a variety of industries, at all levels were surveyed. Each participant had a computer on the desk.

on it. If you are working on a project and have scores of pieces of paper relating to different projects on the desk, you are more likely to face unwanted distractions than if your desk was clear. Is it not reasonable to suggest that if an important letter is hidden under a mountain of paperwork on the desk it will probably not be dealt with? The common sense argument for a clear desk is a strong one, but it is also backed up by research.

Research has shown that a piece of paper on the desk will distract you five times a day. Studies have found that searching for documents on and around a cluttered desk will take up to 45 minutes a day. Those who work from cluttered desks have been found to suffer from more stress than those who work in an organized environment. Seventy percent of respondents to the *Clear Your Desk!* survey admitted that they had missed important opportunities because the relevant information was hidden under a pile of papers on their desks.

Another good reason behind the clear desk comes from looking at the paper-handling habits of successful executives. The message comes across loud and clear from the top *Clear Your Desk!* advocate. Sir Allen Sheppard, Chief Executive of Grand Metropolitan, has a reputation for being ruthless with unnecessary paperwork. He states quite simply, "I never have any paperwork on the desk ... if I saw someone had a mountain of paperwork on the desk with no logic or semblance to it, I would assume they were a bit out of control." Sir John Harvey-Jones humbly states that he tries to get his paperwork done by 9:00 A.M. every day. He recalls:

The registrar of my university had an unbelievably cluttered desk, you had to fight your way into his office, there were piles of paper all over the floor. I couldn't have worked like that—it would have driven me mad. I don't like clutter on the desk, at minimum it may say that the executive is disorganized, it may say something about lack of clarity and it may say someone is not actually coping with the job.

Richard Branson prefers to work at a large table rather than the formal environment of a desk. He receives over 700 letters a week but his table will only have as much on it as is necessary to the project at hand. Gerald Ratner works from a 20 square foot oak desk but he allows very little paperwork to land on it:

It's not what I want to spend my time doing, one of the things I want to achieve in life is enjoying my job and I would not enjoy it if I spent my time doing paperwork, I dislike paperwork. If I walked into someone's office and they had a clear desk it would tell me that the person was well organized.

Anita Roddick prefers to keep her communication oral to reduce the paperwork mountain. She keeps her desk free from all paper but does admit to covering it in ingredients for her potions from all over the world. "There could be anything on it, from nightingale droppings from the Amazon to camomile flowers from France. If someone needs to see me, I need to be able to grab the latest discovery and show it to them." Her colleagues report that she does not work from a desk, she works on the run! Jeffrey Archer recently told a *Sunday Times* journalist, "My desk is probably the tidiest desk you have ever seen. On it are six pencils neatly in a row, six pens neatly in a row, one eraser, one pencil sharpener, one tiny clock. That's it, nothing else gets on the desk."

Professor George Bain, principal of the London Business School, is another executive who keeps his paperwork under control: "I'm a ruthless clear desk man. I would get infuriated if I had to waste my time looking for bits and pieces of paper. When I go home in the evening there is no paper on the desk."

No better testimonial for the clear desk could be received than those from converted paperholics. Many such people have attended Clear Your Desk! seminars. I have met many office workers who regularly surround themselves with clutter—from the first day in their first office. After attending the seminar and clearing their desks they found that those maddening searches among the piles of paper on the desk disappeared and that they are leaving the office earlier without the bulging briefcases, confident in the knowledge that the important paperwork has been dealt with.

THE MYTHS SURROUNDING THE CLUTTERED DESK

Before beginning to look at techniques for controlling desktop disorder we must first examine some of the commonly held beliefs about the cluttered desk. It is these misunderstandings about clutter that lead to the acceptance of the cluttered desk as the norm in most organizations.

Myth: But I know where everything is.
Reality: The more paperwork you hoard on your desk the more time you will spend trying to locate mislaid documents. The first line of defense for the person who works from a cluttered desk is often, "Yes I have a cluttered desk but I can locate any piece of paper within ten seconds." An American study entitled *How People Organize Their Desks* tested this myth by studying two

managers. Both worked for the same company, performing similar jobs but one worked from a cluttered desk and the other from a more organized workspace. Both managers were asked to locate certain documents they both had in common and their searches were timed. Not surprisingly the manager with the cluttered desk took much longer to find things on and around his desk and there were several documents he could not find at all.

The person who works from the cluttered desk is not the person to ask about difficulty in locating documents—he or she will never openly admit it. But if you ask that person's colleagues you will hear such comments as, "I never leave anything on the desk when he's not around because he won't notice it when he gets back" and "She spends half her day trying to find things on the desk." The cluttered desk is made up of a large number of pieces of paper on different subjects, placed on different parts of the desk at different times. These pieces of paper are constantly shuffled around as we add and remove other documents from the desk. As the paperwork builds up on the desk we quickly lose track of where things are.

"But I know where everything is!"

Myth: But I do my job well.

Reality: Working from a cluttered desk does not mean that you cannot do your job well but it does mean that doing a good job will take a lot more time and effort than if your desk was clear. The first class results of people who work from cluttered desks are often compared to the less excellent performance of their colleagues who work from clear desks as proof that clutter doesn't have a negative effect on productivity. The comparison, however, is an unfair one. There are many factors which play a part in job performance, including knowledge, interpersonal skills and intelligence which will enable someone to perform well in spite of a cluttered desk. Einstein was one of those people who achieved great things from a cluttered desk, but who knows what he would have achieved if his desk had been better organized!

"But I do my job well!"

Myth: It's just a difference in personality.

Reality: There are undoubtedly those among us who are meticulously neat and orderly in everything they do and there are those who will always be surrounded by clutter whether at home or in the office. Personality, therefore, will play a part in the build up of paperwork on the desk but the clutter-happy executive will still be unproductive as along as he or she works from a cluttered desk. Dr. Marilyn Davidson, Senior Lecturer in Organizational Psychology at UMIST's School of Management considers that clutter-happy executives may be trying to give the impression to others that they have a lot of work to do:"In the office environment you need to look as if you are busy. So mess on the desk is a way of saying 'I am needed by the company—look how overloaded I am'."

"It's just a difference in personality!"

Myth: I need to keep it on the desk to remind me to do it.
Reality: paperwork left on the desktop to act as a visible reminder usually becomes hidden among the stacks of other "reminders" you have left there. At best if the paperwork remains in your line of vision it will distract you several times before you finally get around to dealing with it. You will place a piece of paper or a document on top of the stack of papers in the in-tray to remind you to do something with it later. However, after several

more items have been placed on top of that particular document it will be forgotten about. It will only be dealt with if you are lucky enough to remember it at the right time or if you come across it by accident while searching for something else.

Myth: A cluttered desk is the sign of a busy mind.
Reality: A cluttered desk is the sign of a disorganized mind and unproductive work patterns. Every piece of paper on the desk apart from the one you are currently dealing with is a sign of a decision not yet made or an action not yet taken. A cluttered desk usually contains a large amount of low pay-off paperwork and even if you are busy it is these quick, easy, fun and comfortable items that receive your attention. As a result you are very busy doing the wrong things.

Myth: There is nothing I can do about it.
Reality: I have often sat in an office and heard its occupants unknowingly encourage paperwork to land on their desks. Your own management style is often the major cause of the avalanche of incoming paperwork and what you do or say can be a sign to others that you can take on their paperwork as well as your own.

Myth: But I'm a creative person.
Reality: This is the most intriguing of all the "clutter" myths. Its origin is unclear but people believe that if they stack lots of paper on the desk and scatter it around their creative juices will magically begin to flow. Stop and think, when do you have your best ideas? If you are like most people they come when you are walking the dog, driving to and from work, at weekends, on holidays, in the shower ... all when you are away from the clutter of the office. If you look back at some of the great creative geniuses over time, Schubert, Bach, Strauss and Jeffrey

Archer, all have had or have clear desk policies. There is one great exception and that was Mozart, who almost always had a cluttered desk but it is doubtful that management at its most creative could ever be compared to the genius of such a composer.

"But I'm a creative person!"

IDENTIFY YOUR PAPER WORKLOAD

Completing this exercise will help you to identify your main paperwork activities and how much time you spend on them. Most people will under-estimate the time they spend on paperwork, whether it is drafting a letter, reading a report or trying to locate documents in the filing cabinet. There are also many activities such as meetings, telephone calls and travelling which indirectly involve paperwork. If you are attending a meeting you may need to read some background paper-work and to jot down items you may want to discuss. During the meeting you will probably need to take notes in order to keep track of what has been said. After the meeting these notes will be used as a basis for any follow up activities.

The questionnaire covers ten categories of paper handling activities. Estimate the time you spend on each category in the typical week and then compare your figures with those taken from a study of office workers at a variety of organizational levels. (See Table 1 on page 19.)

1. How much time do you spend writing in a typical week? Make a list of your writing activities. Your list may include letters, reports, memos, ideas, plans, standard forms and even message slips.

2. How much time do you spend reading? Make a list of all the reading material that normally receives your attention. Your list may include brochures, reports, reference books, manuals, magazines, newsletters and memos.

3. How much time do you spend number crunching? Make a list of the paperwork of this type that you usually deal with. This category ranges from checking invoices and quotations to completing detailed analysis of budgets, costs and sales figures.

4. How much time do you spend each week searching for things on or around the desk? Include the time spent on all those short searches for items located on the desktop, floor, shelves or in your briefcase, desk draws and in-tray. Most office workers will undertake 100-200 of these searches in a week. You must also include the less frequent searches for lost items which waste a lot more of your time.

5. How much mail typically lands on your desk in each week? How long does it take you to process your mail, read it and to decide what action needs to be taken? What types of letters do you receive? Make a list of the categories of mail that normally land on your desk; it may include client enquiries, invoices, junk mail, complaints and inter-office mail.

6. On average how much time do you spend planning in the typical week? What do you use to keep track of your commitments, activities and to-do items? This may include desk diaries, pocket diaries, wall planners, to-do lists, Post-it™ notes and other loose bits of paper.

7. How much time to you spend retrieving documents from your filing system? Office workers open their filing cabinets an average of five times a day to retrieve documents. Many items are located straight away but it has been estimated that about five percent of documents are misfiled and a considerable amount of time is wasted trying to find out where.

8. How much time do you spend giving written instructions to others? Every time you pass on paperwork to someone else there are likely to be some instructions on what to do with it. What proportion of these instructions are written?

9. How long do you spend proofreading material—from letters to memos and reports? Written communications are on average redrafted three times before being dispatched and so would be proofread four times.

10. How much time do you spend filing documents away in your filing cabinet? You first have to make the decision to keep the document and then decide where it should be filed. You may need to search for a correct folder in your filing cabinet or set up a new file to accommodate the item.

Table 1: Average time spent per week on various paper handling activities.

	Average office worker		Your estimate	
	hours	minutes	hours	minutes
1 Writing	6	15		
2 Reading	2	55		
3 Calculating	2	35		
4 Searching	2	15		
5 Mail handling	1	45		
6 Scheduling	1	40		
7 File retrieving	1	25		
8 Delegating	1	-		
9 Proofreading	-	55		
10 Filing	-	50		
Total	21	35		

WHAT IS YOUR CURRENT BACKLOG OF PAPERWORK?

Remember that the average office worker will have a 40 hour backlog of paperwork to deal with. Estimate the time it would take you to work through all the paperwork currently on your desk. Many people when completing this exercise exclude all the junk paperwork on their desk saying ,"I won't spend any time on that." However, junk paperwork does attract your attention and it becomes especially attractive when there is a report you don't want to write or some other uncomfortable job in front of you. Work through the stacks of paper on your desk and estimate how long it will take to deal with each item. A report on your desk might take 30 minutes to read, drafting replies to five letters might take 80 minutes in total, a computer printout might take 15 minutes to analyze, and so on.

How many hours of unfinished paperwork do you currently have on the desk?

It is now time to turn your attention to the problems that are caused by the build up of paperwork on your desk.

CHAPTER TWO

Paperwork Problems

I don't like clutter, at minimum it may say that the executive is disorganized, it may say something about lack of clarity and it may say he [or she] is not actually coping with the job.

— Sir John Harvey-Jones

THIS CHAPTER EXPLORES the problems that we all face when we allow paperwork to build up on our desks. You will certainly have experienced the frustrating searches for mislaid paperwork; the inability to concentrate on any one project when you have other paperwork on your desk clamoring for your attention; the realization that you have missed an important opportunity as you discover forgotten paperwork at the bottom of the in-tray and the feelings of stress as you suffocate under a large backlog of paperwork. You are not alone in the struggle with unnecessary paperwork; look around you in the office and you will see others experiencing the same problems. The report that should have been on your desk last week is still in draft form buried on the desk of a colleague; the client order form that you should be processing is lying at the bottom of another's in-tray; phone messages taken in your absence have not reached you because they were scribbled down on pieces of paper and accidentally discarded or mislaid...the list goes on.

HOW CLUTTERED IS YOUR DESK?

The questionnaire below will help you to recognize the signs of out of control paperwork. Each time your answer is "yes" put a check in the box on the right hand side of the page.

1. While sitting at your desk do you ever feel completely overwhelmed by the backlog of paperwork facing you? ☐

2. Do you frequently worry about unfinished paperwork on your desk, when you are away from the office? ☐

3. Is there so much paperwork on the desk that you have to find another clear space when you want to tackle an important project? ☐

4. Do you have days in the office when you have been extremely busy dealing with paperwork but don't feel as if you have achieved anything constructive? ☐

5. Do you often fill your briefcase with paperwork to deal with at home? ☐

6. Do you often stay late in the office to try and catch up on the backlog of paperwork? ☐

7. Do you spend too much time "fire-fighting" because the paperwork has not been dealt with effectively? ☐

8. While working on one project are you often distracted by other paperwork around you on your desk? ☐

9. Do you ever find paperwork on your desk that you have forgotten about and it is too late to do anything with it? ☐

10. Do you spend too much time looking for paperwork on or around your desk? ☐

11. Do you often put off uncomfortable paperwork and deal with lower pay-off, but more interesting items? ☐

12. Do you sometimes miss important opportunities because you have been too busy to deal with the paperwork? ☐

13. Do you often handle paperwork several times before finally deciding what to do with it? ☐

14. Do you face too many interruptions from your colleagues rushing towards your desk with paperwork for your attention? ☐

15. Do you always keep paperwork moving or does it tend to build up on your desk? ☐

Questionnaire Analysis
Give yourself one point for each box you have checked.

Score 0-5
You would appear to have your paperwork under control. However, the questionnaire may have helped you to identify certain areas in which you need to fine tune your paper handling skills. When you have read the remainder of this chapter go through the questionnaire a second time.

Score 6-10

The majority of the readers of this book will fit into this category. You probably notice that your paperwork problems increase as you become busier. Like many people, you may believe that the problems you face are beyond your control. However, recognizing that a problem exists is the first step towards controlling it. The second step is simple—Clear Your Desk!

Score 11-15

You are a committed paperholic; you almost certainly do not need a questionnaire to tell you that you have some serious problems. Your bad paper handling habits will have been built up over a number of years along with a litany of excuses used to justify them. The battle against paperwork will be tough for you but the rewards will be high.

EXECUTIVES WHO WORK AT CLUTTERED DESKS WORK LONGER HOURS

Gerald Ratner does not admire the executive who spends long hours shuffling paperwork around the desk:

> *I went up to someone in my office who had a mountain of paperwork on the desk and [he] said, "I can't go on vacation because I have all this paperwork to clear. If I go on vacation, when I come back there will be even more!" I was unimpressed with that because I felt that if he couldn't organize a holiday with his wife and kids for two weeks then he was really not capable of running that department.*

At the end of the last chapter you will have calculated the backlog of paperwork currently lying on your desktop. If your backlog is close to that of the average office worker you will have a 40 hour paperwork mountain waiting for your attention. Stop and think for a moment. In any one day you will only spend approximately eight hours in the office. With forty hours of work but only eight hours in which to get through it you face a seemingly impossible task. You may even have a paperwork backlog of much more than 40 hours.

A large part of our day is taken up with formal meetings and informal communications with others. On top of that is the never ending stream of new paperwork that needs to be tackled. There is always pressure on us to catch up, to recover our control of the situation. The natural reaction is to spend more time in the office to do just that. When 5:00 P.M. comes around, we look at our in-tray and discover that there are still several important items that need to be tackled, and as a matter of habit we pick up the phone and announce that we will be home late again. Seven P.M. arrives and we have begun to make some impression on the backlog when we suddenly remember that report we were supposed to prepare. A pile of background documents are crammed into our already full briefcase and we head for home. By 10 P.M. we are lying asleep in front of the TV with pen in one hand, draft report in the other.

The above scenario is one which is repeated by executives worldwide struggling to cope with the overload of work. Paper spills from the desk into their private lives, and their families and friends are ignored as evenings and weekends are spent pouring over paperwork. Some executives can be heard to claim quite proudly that it has been many years since they last took a real vacation; others with greater concern for their families promise themselves that after this project or that crisis is dealt with they will spend more time at home, but some other project or crisis always moves in to take its place.

It is an unfortunate fact that many companies actively encourage their people to work long hours. One company I visited, however, sends its senior managers around the office at 5:30 P.M. on Friday evenings to send everyone home. That company's philosophy is that if employees cannot do their jobs in the time given, then they are either hopelessly disorganized and need further training or they are not capable of doing the job in the first place.

The real problem of course does not lie in the amount of paperwork that lands on the desk—we could in fact spend 24 hours of each day dealing with it—but in how effectively and efficiently we deal with it. We might deal with a report more efficiently by eliminating

A cluttered desk means longer hours.

any distracting paperwork from our desks or by spending less time searching for background documents. However, the report may be considered unnecessary by those who receive it, so the paperwork might have been dealt with more effectively by discarding it in the first place.

A CLUTTERED DESK MEANS YOU WILL GET LESS DONE!

In the last chapter the myth that a cluttered desk means a busy and productive mind was exploded. The reality is that working in a cluttered environment will have a negative effect on your productivity. Imagine that you are in a situation requiring you to delegate paperwork that needs to be done quickly and you have the choice of two people of equal ability, one with a clear desk, the other surrounded by a mountain of paperwork. Who would you delegate to?

The more unfinished paperwork on the desk the more difficult it becomes to see through the clutter exactly what your priorities are. It is almost the definitive case of not being able to see the forest for the trees. In the Clear Your Desk! survey almost 70 percent of the respondents admitted to missing important opportunities because the relevant paperwork was hidden on their desks. The best salesperson in the world cannot even begin to sell if he or she has lost client enquiry details under a stack of papers on the desk. Sir Allen Sheppard works from a clear desk and gives this reason: "If I simply had piles of paper on the desk and I didn't know whether I was sitting on something important, I would get very irritated and the best way to avoid irritation is to ensure that it never happens."

The more paperwork we unnecessarily hoard on our desks the greater the probability that our time will be spent on items which are not going to give us a high pay-off. We waste time on documents that should have been discarded as soon as they arrived on the desk while our important paperwork is left undone. Most of us acquired the habit of picking up, reading and putting down pieces of paper several times before finally deciding how to act on them. This is a major time-stealer and techniques for combating it will be discussed later.

The most productive way to tackle paperwork is to decide what item to tackle next based on its expected pay-off. However, working from a cluttered desk encourages a tendency to work from the top of the nearest stack downwards or distraction by interesting paperwork scattered about the desk.

Whether or not the important paperwork is completed at a cluttered desk is often a matter of luck rather than conscious decision. Often when we do have important items in front of us they do not get our full attention because we are suffering from a condition known as paper fatigue. Our eyes glaze over as a result of the sheer volume of paper that passes in front of them and we fail to spot key points in letters, we fill out forms incorrectly and we fail to retain most of what we read.

A CLUTTERED DESK IS A BREEDING GROUND FOR CRISES

Is there paperwork on your desk at this very moment that if not dealt with quickly will result in a crisis? It might be a report that needs to be read and acted upon, a client letter that requires a speedy response or a paper essential to the successful completion of a project. Think back over the crises you have faced in the past month. How many were due to the ineffective handling of paperwork? Incorrectly processing paperwork the first time around or losing paperwork that requires immediate action under a pile of other papers on the desk can lead to a crisis. The longer important paperwork remains on the desk the greater the chance that a crisis will develop. One person who attended the Clear Your Desk! seminar recounted how he had received an order from an important client with a strict delivery deadline. Instead of being passed on directly to the distribution department the order form lay untouched at the bottom of his in-tray for several weeks. The delivery due date arrived and the client called to confirm the exact time of delivery. All hell broke loose: the salesman had to go to the storeroom, check that the item was in stock and make the delivery himself. The result was three wasted hours. The story will not be unfamiliar to most of you. The Clear Your Desk! survey found that people spent an average of five-and-a-half hours a week fire-fighting because of paperwork problems. That seemingly harmless piece of paper that lands on your desk today, requiring only two minutes' work may develop into a three hour monster if ignored.

All of the top executives I interviewed tackle paperwork almost as soon as it lands on their desks. Professor George Bain of the London Business School advises:

> *I try and handle a piece of paper only once. I will go through the mail dealing with the routine, leaving aside anything that requires further thought, if it is only me who has to think about it, I deal with it pretty fast, otherwise you would get submerged under a mountain of paper. I try to keep things flowing across the desk.*

Those of us who constantly work from cluttered desks get dragged into the crisis cycle. While our time is taken up fighting fires, lying unfinished on the desk is the paperwork that will lead to the next crisis. Then as we rush off to deal with that crisis more fires are beginning to burn on the desk. Fire-fighters are always part arsonists.

The "fire-fighter"

DISTRACTIONS, DISTRACTIONS, DISTRACTIONS

The more pieces of paper we hoard on our desks the more distractions we will face. It has been estimated that each piece of paper we hoard on our desks will distract us up to five times a day. What happens when we have ten, twenty, one hundred, even several hundred pieces of paper on the desk clamoring for our attention? Our distraction level goes through the roof. We cannot concentrate on one project for any length of time without being sidetracked by other paperwork lying on the desk.

A typical distraction might be as follows. It is ten o'clock and you have just started work on a report. Ten minutes later you experience a slight lapse in concentration and out of the corner of your eye, you spot a letter which needs attention. Before you realize what you are doing you have picked up the letter saying to yourself, "I'll have to send a reply this afternoon but I need to check a few details with Bill first." The letter is placed on the desk beside you and you get back to the report. A short while later the letter catches your attention a second time and you remind yourself of some further details you need to discuss with Bill. By the time you have finished the report you have faced several more of these minor distractions and paperwork that should have taken an hour to complete has taken twice as long.

Each time you face a distraction you waste time in two ways. Firstly, there is the time spent dealing with the paperwork that has caused the distraction. Secondly, in going back to your original project you have to go through a warm up period to build up your concentration to a productive level again.

Now consider the major distractions. A small lapse in concentration occurs and suddenly you are distracted by a Post-it™ note reminding you to call someone. Without having made a conscious decision to change the focus of your attention you are in the middle of a telephone conversation. Then as you put down the phone an interesting magazine article shouts at you from the top of the in-tray and you pick it up. The end result is that the paperwork that you were originally working on lies unfinished on the desk.

The figure below illustrates the distraction process. Our concentration level does not remain constant but varies over time. We all have a "distraction threshold" below which level, if there is paperwork around us on the desk, we will be distracted by it.

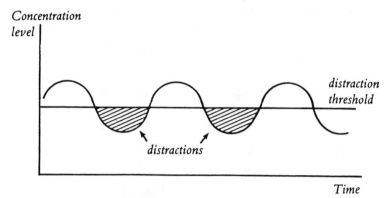

The distraction process

Many people have so much clutter on their desks that they end up being distracted from their distractions and they leave a trail of unfinished paperwork on the desk. Each piece of unfinished paperwork then becomes a potential distractor in the future because every time we spot it we are reminded that it needs to be tackled.

Each piece of paper on the desk will distract you up to five times a day!

LOSING THINGS

Working with someone who has to do a head dive into the in-tray to find something they want to talk to you about clearly demonstrates that something is wrong.

— Sir Allen Sheppard

The phone rings, it is an important client: "Have you followed up on the letter I sent you a couple of weeks ago?" You reply, "Oh yes I have it here on my desk," a frantic search ensues and a couple of minutes later, with the client growing ever more impatient on the other end of the phone, you have to abandon the search. "Can I get back to you on it?" You then spend the next 20 minutes searching for the letter, while your client rings your competitor who doesn't lose things on the desk.

It has been shown that the manager working at his or her desk will change the focus of his or her attention on average, once every ten minutes. So that manager would typically be involved in about 50 activities during the course of the day. If even half of these activities involve paperwork it will mean stopping work 25 times to locate documents on the desk. The more cluttered your desk the longer these searches will take. The Clear Your Desk! survey shows that people spend an average of 22 minutes a day just looking for things on or around the desk and that does not include time spent searching through the filing system. That 22 minutes is made up of a large number of short searches, which involve going through a stack of papers until the correct item is found, and also a smaller number of longer searches of the type, "I left it here yesterday, where can it possibly have gone?"

Spending five percent of your time searching for things on the desktop is not something that would immediately worry you; however, 22 minutes a day over a lifetime in the office adds up to 400 working days. On that basis you could justify taking a year off work just to learn how to clear your desk. From a corporate viewpoint the time spent by employees looking for things is very expensive. A company employing 1000 office workers pays out $1,425,000 in salary every year to people who are trying to locate paperwork. We must also add the revenue forgone because of important information that is irretrievably lost on the desk. There is no way of calculating the cost of opportunities that have passed us by because of paperwork that has been mislaid.

We have already exploded the "But I know where everything is" myth. A piece of paper placed in one spot on the desk will not remain there for long. As you search for other documents underneath, it will be transferred to another stack and several other items will be piled on top of it. If you played back a video recording of a desk at high speed you would see documents moving between several different stacks or piles of paper on the desk. Rather than using the maxim, "A place for everything and everything in its place," to organize our desks most of us follow the principle "everything all over the place." In the middle of a telephone conversation you are required to take down a few details. Where and on what do you write them? On a special page you use for keeping track of communications with that person? Not likely. Most probably you will scribble the details down on whatever piece of paper happens to be in front of you at the time. It might be a computer printout, a fax or a letter. What happens when you have finished dealing with that letter on which you scribbled down the details? It is filed away or transferred to the desk of someone else. Two days later you are searching for the details, you remember writing them down on a piece of paper but you can't find it. Many of you are probably familiar with recovering a piece of paper from the waste basket and uncrumpling it to find an important telephone number in the corner.

FOUND IT!

*We spend 22 minutes a day just looking for things
on and around the desk!*

WORKING FROM A CLUTTERED DESK
YOU WILL END UP DOING THE WORK OF OTHERS

You are busy tackling paperwork at the desk when a colleague walks into the office. "I have a problem with this, boss, can you give me some input?" You are too busy dealing with yesterday's backlog of paperwork so you look up and say, "Leave it with me, I'll look at it later, I'm very busy right now." The paperwork lands on your desk and reverse delegation has taken place. The responsibility for moving the project on to the next stage is now firmly in your lap. Later that afternoon your colleague will pop his head around the door and ask, "Have you had a chance to look at it yet?" You reply that you will see to it as soon as you have the time, a scenario known as "supervising the boss."

Working from a cluttered desk you may notice a line of people at your office door waiting for you to tackle their paperwork. You of course have your own paperwork to deal with but you can't see through the clutter where the important paperwork lies. As a result you often end up dealing with low pay-off, urgent paperwork that has just arrived rather than the high pay-off paperwork at the bottom of the in-tray.

The Clear Your Desk! survey found that people face an average of eight unwanted paperwork interruptions a day and the most common reaction to the interruption is, "Leave it with me." You should be sending people away but you already have so much on the desk that one more piece of paper doesn't seem to make much difference.

Those who work from clear desks jealously guard the sanctity of their workspace. Nothing is allowed on the desktop without its pay-off being evaluated.

Working from a cluttered desk you are always catching up on yesterday's workload. You never get the chance to plan tomorrow's paperwork, to stand back and ask, "What should I be doing here?" As a result the urgent items of your colleagues often receive your attention while your own important paperwork lies untouched on the desk.

PROCRASTINATION LEADS TO CLUTTER LEADS TO PROCRASTINATION

It is 9:00 A.M. and you have just arrived in the office. You sit down at your desk and spot an important report which really should be completed today. You pick it up and tell yourself for the tenth time that week that you are going to finish it. As you review what you have written to date the morning mail arrives and the report is put aside. There are several items which receive your attention immediately. It is 10:30 A.M. by the time you pick up the report again. You have written two sentences when you spot a magazine article on the desk. The article would not normally be of interest, in fact it really belongs in the trash, but it is an infinitely more attractive prospect than finishing the report. Having read the article you are again faced with the prospect of tackling the report. The stack of low pay-off paperwork in the in-tray suddenly assumes great importance and you really must deal with some of those items. The report still remains unfinished by 3:00 P.M. when an urgent but non-important fax arrives which you decide to deal with straight away. The report once again is pushed aside—you won't have the time to finish it today even if you started now, so you decide to tackle it first thing tomorrow morning....

Each piece of paper lying on the desk represents a decision not yet made or an action not yet taken. The build up of paperwork encourages us to procrastinate further. Uncomfortable paperwork such as a report we don't want to analyze or a letter we don't want to write can be conveniently hidden among the stack of papers on the desktop. While we are procrastinating we can get busy on the quick, easy, fun and comfortable paperwork of which there is an abundance on the desk. The perfect way to ease our conscience.

The Clear Your Desk! survey found that 43 percent of individuals handle paperwork several times before finally deciding what to do with it. Putting things off becomes a habit. The paperwork that should be acted upon immediately is delayed while we await more information and the paperwork that should be discarded is left on the desktop because we think we might get a chance to deal with it some other time. Professor George Bain has a rule that everything that comes in during the day goes out on the same day. "I think one of the main ways of creating work is to put aside small jobs. I find that if it's something you do right away, then bang, that's it, whereas if you put it aside you create a whole pile of jobs for yourself."

STRESS AND THE CLUTTERED DESK

The medical textbooks define stress as occurring when the demands of the situation outweigh our perceived capabilities to meet those demands. So if you walked out of your front door in the morning to find a lion in your garden ready to pounce, your stress levels would immediately increase. The demands of the situation would be greater than your perceived ability to cope. In the same way a cluttered desk leads to a stress reaction. You are faced with an average backlog of 40 hours of paperwork yet in any one day you will only have a few hours in which to deal with it. Furthermore it seems that every time you sit down to tackle the backlog you are interrupted by colleagues bringing more paperwork for your attention, not to mention those frustrating searches for mislaid information. You always seem to be catching up, never in control. You leave the office every evening knowing that there are important items lying on the desk which should have been tackled and you lie awake at night worrying about them. Many people report being so overwhelmed by the mountain of paperwork on their desks that they find some other space in which to work.

Those people who frequently work from cluttered desks will recognize the "paperwork panic attack." It can be sparked off by a paperwork interruption when you are trying to finish something important or just by looking at the desk and realizing how much you have to do. The "alarm button" in the brain, the hypothalamus, goes off and causes adrenalin to be released into the bloodstream. The heart rate accelerates and pumps blood to the muscles, which become flexed, ready for action. Your blood pressure rises and you begin to breathe more quickly to increase the oxygen supply to the blood. You clench your teeth and begin to perspire ... but for what? This stress response is appropriate for dealing with the lion in your front garden where you need to be ready for "fight or flight," but not for dealing with paperwork on the desk. The body can recover from occasional paper panic attacks, but if they are persistent you may begin to experience headaches, stomach ulcers, even heart attacks and alcohol dependency. Cluttered desks create a hazard to your health.

Cluttered desks lead to stress!

CHAPTER THREE

Eliminating Unnecessary Paperwork

Communication is a byword at the Body Shop, so ultimately anything that facilitates it must work for me. But I really have a problem with paper. I feel once thoughts are on paper, they can be thrown away. Much better to keep them on the wing and flying around in the air via the spoken word.

— Anita Roddick

ALL PAPERWORK IMPOSES some burden upon us. This burden becomes unnecessary when we have to deal with items which should never have arrived on the desk in the first place. Throughout the day your colleagues charge towards your desk with paperwork for your attention. As you struggle to cope with that workload additional items arrive from your paperholic boss. Bureaucratic paperwork in the form of reports, memos and standard forms provide further obstacles to effective action. Sir John Harvey-Jones is strongly in favor of burdening people as little as possible with paperwork. "I look upon paperwork as not being anything to do with the running of a job and that is actually Naval training, where if you were involved in paperwork you were considered not to be working. Working was being with your people." Admiral Joseph Metcalfe of the U.S. Navy is another passionate believer in the "action not paperwork" principle. Exasperated with the 20 tons of paper and filing cabinets being loaded on his destroyer, he was heard to declare that if engaged in battle, he would fire paper at the enemy. His rationale presumably was that the enemy, like all other human beings, would get so bogged down in the mountain of bureaucratic paperwork being fired at them that they would get nothing useful done in the way of retaliation. "Paperwork is the absolute enemy of industry," declares Gerald Ratner, and he is ruthless in eliminating unnecessary paperwork.

This chapter looks at techniques for reducing the flow of unnecessary paperwork across the desk. Many elements of that flow will be under your direct control and the techniques can be put into practice straight away. It is unlikely that you will succeed in eliminating a standard form or a company-wide report single-handedly, but you can make a significant contribution by being part of a *Clear Your Desk!* committee formed to look at ways of reducing paperwork. No matter how far down the organizational ladder you lie, you can still contribute constructively to this process.

REDUCING UNNECESSARY REPORTS

Napoleon had an admirable attitude towards reports. It was the tradition of his time that generals would produce a written report on each battle they fought. Napoleon, however, would discard these reports unread because he believed that if anything important had happened he would already have heard of it by word of mouth. In the 1990's you would do well to follow Napoleon's example. Managers in any large organization will tell you that the majority of reports they receive are unnecessary but at the same time will say that most of the reports they produce are important. Some of the forces that lead to the proliferation of unnecessary reports are discussed below.

The decision-avoidance report
The writers of these reports are trying to avoid taking action or making a decision. Instead of saying "let's do it" and risking the possibility of making a mistake they put all of their time and effort into producing a report. If anyone questions them about the progress they are making on the project they can always reply, "I'm working on it, I'll let you have a report on it soon." The report is often delayed as they seek out more and more information. When it is finally completed the report is

placed on someone else's desk in order to pass on the problem. Sir Allen Sheppard detests reports that, "are just an attempt to shuffle a problem around the office," and prefers his executives to act rather than "play it safe and write a huge report."

The design-junkie report

The design-junkie report places greater emphasis on how the report looks rather than what it contains. Advances in desktop publishing have led to the proliferation of this type of report. The writer drafts and redrafts several times because "the graph would look better in another format" or because "the font is not quite right." There will usually be a stack of abandoned papers on the desk of the design junkie which have not quite passed the presentation quality test. The final result is a report that looks good but contains very little useful information and is likely to be late. Despite this the report will be distributed to more people than is necessary so that they might admire its aesthetic quality.

The self-protection report

The chief purpose of the self-protection report is to absolve the writer of any blame in the case of something going wrong. An interesting story that illustrates the problems caused by this type of report comes from NASA. During the early flights of the U.S. space shuttle there were serious problems caused by the heat-protective tiles falling off during re-entry into the earth's atmosphere. Two teams had been assigned to the tile development program but they were located several hundred miles apart. For two years the major goal of this program had been to resolve the adhesive problem, yet there was no solution in sight. A new manager with a reputation for straight talking was brought in to rectify the situation and he soon realized that there was absolute chaos on the program. Every Monday morning he would arrive at work and something would have gone seriously wrong during the weekend testing. By Tuesday morning one of the groups would have produced a 100-page report outlining why the problem was not their fault and would lay the blame firmly on the shoulders of the second group. By Wednesday morning the second group would have produced a report of the same length refuting the allegations. This pattern of events had been repeated every week for the past two years.

Deciding that drastic action was needed to resolve the situation, the manager flew both teams to a neutral location one Friday afternoon and locked them in a hotel room for seven hours. The same thing happened the next week and the week after that. Within six weeks the problem had been completely solved. The two teams had begun to communicate with each other. Their defense mechanisms broken down, they had begun to work towards a common goal. Their new manager was later reported saying that it was easy to "bullshit" in a 100-page report but practically impossible to do so face-to-face.

The loquacious report
This type of report is characterized by its length. Such reports are often evidence that the writer has not fully grasped the subject and has therefore included a large amount of superfluous material. The report talks around the subject without ever really getting to the point. If asked "what are you really trying to say here" the author of the report would invariably be lost for words. Almost as trying for report readers is too much information. Many "experts" will produce bumper reports to impress their colleagues with their knowledge of a particular

subject. The important points however are hidden behind a torrent of words. Sir John Harvey-Jones is a very strong believer in short reports: "The most successful committee I ever ran was one which took no report which was longer than one page." He recalls, "It was absolute murder to get people to adhere to that, but the great advantage of being brief is that you get to the nub of the problem."

REPORT REDUCTION ACTION PLAN

This action plan is suitable for both individuals who want to reduce the number of reports that land on their desks and Clear Your Desk! committees who are trying to reduce the wastage of organizational resources in the reporting process. The objectives of the action plan are twofold:

(a) To eliminate unnecessary reports and the time wasted producing and reading them.

(b) To ensure that the important reports are accurate, consistent and concise, and go to the right people at the right time.

The impetus for the action plan should come from the top down in the organization. Each manager should, where possible, encourage those below him or her to present information verbally rather than in a long report. A reward scheme should be set up to reinforce the use of effective reporting.

---

1. Collect reports

Gather together all the reports you receive on a regular basis along with the special reports you have recently asked for. Calculate the number of report pages that land on your desk in a typical month.

The average reading speed for light material is about 250 words per minute or about two minutes per page. Based on this figure how long would it take you to read every page of every report you receive? It always takes us longer to read reports than we imagine. At average reading speed, in a ten hour day we would only get through three, 100-page reports. How much time can you afford to spend reading reports?

If you are evaluating all the reports in the organization, calculate how many pages of reports are produced every month. How long would it take to read each report and all of its copies?

2. Report reading patterns

Take each report in turn and ask yourself, "Have I read this report?" "Should I read it?" If you answer no in both cases then have your name taken off the circulation list. If you are the only person who has received this report, then its writer has put in a lot of time and effort for nothing. Why did you ask for this report in the first place? Do not ask for similar reports in the future.

If you only read certain parts of a report such as the summary, conclusions or sections relevant to your function, ask that only these parts of the report are sent to you in future. Does the person who writes the report realize that you don't read the full report? Would this affect the time and effort that goes into its production?

What percentage of the reported information

that lands on your desk is actually read? What percentage of all the reports produced in the organization are read?

3. Reports and decision-making

For each report ask yourself what effect it has had on your decisions.

If you regularly receive a report but have been reading it merely out of interest, then take your name off the circulation list and concentrate your efforts on higher pay-off paperwork.

If the report affects the way you do your job only when something extraordinary happens, introduce the exception reporting principle. Define with the person who produces the report under what exceptional circumstances you wish to receive a copy of the report.

What percentage of the reports that land on your desk have a major effect on your decision-making?

4. Economic feasibility

What does it cost to produce each report? Include the cost of gathering information, writing and duplicating it. What value do you place on the report? If you had to pay for the information what value would you place on it? Is the total value of the report as determined by all its readers greater than the cost of its production? If the cost is greater than the perceived value, the report should be eliminated.

Alternatively, ways of reducing the production cost could be explored. The scope of the report could be narrowed or its means of production made more efficient.

What is the total cost to the organization of report production? You have already calculated the percentage of reports that do not have a major effect on your decision making. Based on this figure, what is the cost of unnecessary report production for your organization?

5. Is there an oral alternative?

Is it absolutely essential that the information contained in the report is transmitted in writing? What would be the result of substituting a face-to-face meeting, a telephone call or a presentation for the report? In most cases verbal information is superior to written communication. You can convey your message in a more persuasive manner and gain instant feedback to your ideas. A lengthy report on the other hand might lie on someone's desk for weeks and when they do get around to reading it they might miss the key points.

Sir Allen Sheppard prefers to get his message across verbally. "At Grand Metropolitan we prefer to talk to each other rather than write to each other."

Richard Branson lives the same message at Virgin. Worldwide, there are about 80 key executives in the Virgin group and Branson tries to talk to each one of them by telephone once a week. This emphasis on verbal communication must reduce the number of reports that land on his desk by several hundred pieces of paper a month.

Sir John Harvey-Jones prefers face-to-face communication in order to breathe life into the subjects, "I don't like people who write long reports. I prefer presentations. I like to see people jumping up and down and using flip charts."

The power of verbal communication is also important to Anita Roddick, "Communication is a byword at the Body Shop, so ultimately anything that facilitates it must work for me. But I really have a problem with paper. I feel once thoughts are on paper, they can be thrown away. Much better to keep them on the wing and flying around in the air via the spoken word."

6. Is the information available elsewhere?
Can the information in the report be located in another report or in raw form? If you can locate the raw data and interpret it satisfactorily then the report should be eliminated. Does the writer of the report duplicate the efforts of others who produce slightly differing reports from the same information?

7. The information gap
What questions do you want answered by each report? Does the report answer those questions in a satisfactory manner? If not, why not? Has there been a change in your circumstances that render the report unnecessary? For example, your job may have changed slightly so that you no longer have responsibility over a certain area. If there is a large gap between the information required and the information provided, you should talk to the author of the report about narrowing that gap. If that person cannot provide the necessary information, the report should be eliminated.

It sometimes happens that the report contains high quality information, but it arrives too late to be of any use. Is it worth the extra time and effort required to make the report more timely? If it is not, eliminate it.

8. Report format
Are all reports produced according to a house style? Do you find yourself wasting time trying to find a report's conclusions or other key sections? Do you find yourself losing your way due to

confusing heading styles? Are you confused by the myriad of graph formats in reports you receive? The Clear Your Desk! committee should lay down format guidelines for report production under the following headings: (a) contents lists; (b) headings; (c) notation; (d) pagination; (e) charts and tables; (f) conclusions and recommendations.

9. Report retention
Working through your stack of reports ask yourself, how soon does this report become obsolete? Do you refer to each report only once and then file it away? If you threw away each report would you be able to locate another copy if for any reason you needed to look at it again? Does everyone who receives a copy of the report file it away? How many reports do you have in your filing system at this moment that belong in the trash? Set up a discard schedule for each report.

10. Writing reports
When writing reports keep the above nine steps in mind. If you write regular reports find out if they are being read and what effect they have on the actions of others. Each time you are asked to write a report find out what questions the report is required to answer. Could you save time and get your message across more effectively by presenting the information orally? By the time the reader gets your report will he or she already have made a decision on the problem, thereby rendering your report unnecessary? Don't waste your time writing self-protection and decision-avoidance reports, nobody will read them.

STAMPING OUT STANDARD FORMS

It is difficult to imagine any organization operating without a multitude of standard forms. Forms to authorize, to claim, to estimate, to follow up, to identify, to instruct, to order, to record, to request, to schedule, to transfer ...

Forms are always produced with the stated intention of helping someone do a better job and there are many forms that do achieve that. A well-designed form can guide you through a complex task and ensure that important elements are not overlooked. Information can be transferred in a format that can easily be understood by others and on one piece of paper. Benefits aside, we could all produce a long list of forms used in our organizations that make the job more difficult to do well. Design faults may mean that the form is impossible to follow or the language ambiguous or unintelligible. Many forms ask for information that will never be used or that can easily be located elsewhere. Then there are the forms whose correct completion has become more important than getting the job done.

It is an unfortunate fact that most people who introduce standard forms do not have to spend many stress-filled hours completing them and are immune from their other ill effects. "Forms drive me mad," exclaims Sir John Harvey-Jones. "They are almost always written for the benefit of the form compiler rather than the poor sod who has to fill them out. They invariably ask for too much information or they don't have enough space for you to say what you want to say."

When considering the introduction of a form, the compiler is faced with a problem that needs to be solved and focuses on how to solve that problem with a single sheet of paper. A year later, however, the form has become a monster and is generating thousands of pieces of paper and soaking up hundreds of hours of working time. In the U.K., over two billion government forms and leaflets are used by the public each year.

The costs in use of a form always eclipse the design and printing costs. Studies have shown that for every dollar spent on printing forms, 40 dollars or more are spent on distributing, processing, correcting errors, storing and destroying them. This is a good rule of thumb to follow when considering the introduction of a new form. Does the cost in use, which is the printing cost x 40, outweigh the benefits that is hoped the form will bring about? The Ministry of Agriculture, Fisheries and Food recently found a form which cost 45 cents to print whereas sending it out, checking it and following up queries cost $7.99, a ratio of 1:177. Another U.K. government department estimated that the cost of correcting errors on one of its forms was in the region of $1,283 million annually.

Is the form really necessary?

The introduction of some forms can enter the realms of the ridiculous. One journalist on a recent trip to India was required to complete a form in triplicate just to make a telephone call from a post office. Another form I came across in a U.S. organization was to be used in case of telephone bomb threats. There were no less than 60 items to be checked off, including the name and address of the terrorist, who presumably would be asked to hold while the paperwork was being completed. The award for the most unnecessary form ever invented, in my experience, however, must go to an item called the truckers daily log. In the 1970's it was illegal for American truckers to drive for more than ten hours in a single day. The U.S. Department of Transportation duly introduced a form to ensure that the law was not breached. Each trucker was obliged to fill in this form every 15 minutes whether or not they were driving. The result was that the department was faced with an avalanche of over a billion pieces of paper a year, an amount which would have produced a stack several miles high. The form had been in use for several years before someone realized that the information it requested neither identified possible violators of the ten hour rule nor helped in their prosecution.

It will never be easy to eliminate unnecessary forms. There is always fierce resistance from the person or department that introduced the form; a long list of reasons will be put forward as to why the elimination of the form will result in chaos. Often the people who suffer most because of the form and who could come up with the best ideas for an alternative are suspicious of change and keep quiet. People who take on the job of reducing bureaucratic paperwork, therefore, need to have both the influence to 'break down a few doors' and the trust of their colleagues.

Gerald Ratner tells the story of a purge of unnecessary forms after his takeover of the H Samuel group. The problem was that

> *when we bought H Samuel they had a lot of forms to fill in and a lot of paperwork that nobody actually knew what it was for. They were just completing it because management wanted a ridiculous amount of information. We want people serving customers, we're very much against paperwork. H Samuel had an office in every shop for the managers and they didn't get out of the office until the middle of the*

week, because they spent Monday, Tuesday and half of Wednesday filling out forms and checking stock.

Gerald Ratner's solution was very effective:

We went in and smashed the walls of the offices down and created more showroom space for the customers. Now the managers are out on Monday morning because we threw all the paperwork away. We don't have any forms that are not absolutely vital. We do not ask our people to fill in anything to give us any information that is not totally essential.

Marcus Sieff instigated a paperwork control program at Marks & Spencer in the 1950's. The high cost of bureaucracy was eating into the profits of the company so a paperwork reduction drive entitled "Operation Simplification" was launched. The program lasted for three years and during that time 26 million pieces of unnecessary paper were eliminated and 1,000 filing cabinets which were no longer needed were sold off.

Early on in the project, Sieff came across a form commonly known as the pink slip. This form was used in triplicate detailing goods inwards. Sieff discovered that all the information asked for by the form could easily be located elsewhere and he proposed a trial elimination in four of the stores. The chief accountant was up in arms predicting that chaos would result if the forms were not used, but Sieff operated on the principle, "If in doubt throw it out." You could always bring a form back but until it was gone you would never know if it was really necessary in the first place. The form was eliminated for one month and after that period he went to its users and asked them how they had coped. They were all delighted with the form's disappearance and begged him not to bring it back. The pink slip was eventually eliminated in all the stores and this move alone saved six million pieces of paper a year.

In 1982, in the U.K., The Review of Administrative Forms in Government, coordinated by Sir Derek Rayner, saw civil servants from eight departments put 93 different forms under the microscope. As a result more than half of them were redesigned and a quarter withdrawn. Within five years the estimated savings from the review of forms was in the region of £14 million ($26 million).

The common element behind these success stories is ruthlessness. Half-hearted attempts to get rid of unnecessary forms will never work. Sir Derek Rayner advised that civil servants should occasionally "tear up some forms in the interest of better administration." It is with that thought that you should begin the Form Reduction Action Plan.

FORM REDUCTION ACTION PLAN

This action plan can be carried out by an individual or a Clear Your Desk! committee depending on the size of your organization. The objectives of the exercise are straightforward, to achieve a major reduction in the amount of time people spend unnecessarily compiling, processing, correcting errors in and storing forms. The guidelines below are no more than advanced common sense, but if implemented properly will bring enormous financial savings, reductions in staff stress levels and a better service to customers.

1. Publicize the form reduction process

The process might be launched by the chief executive tearing up an unnecessary form at a company conference. If you are setting up a Clear Your Desk! committee it should have a senior manager at its head, a person with the ability to break through any bureaucratic barriers that might stand in the way of success. Some companies have set up rolling committees whereby the directors from the different functions take it in turns to chair the committee which then examines the forms in their own areas.

Place an article in your company newsletter encouraging people to come forward with ideas for improvements in forms and for ways of doing their jobs that don't involve forms. When people do come forward, listen to what they have to say and implement their ideas. A reward scheme should be set up for individuals and departments who come up with the best suggestions.

2. Set a target for the elimination of unnecessary forms

A 50 percent reduction of forms used is an achievable target for one year. Keep people informed as to how the program is proceeding and if the target is reached company wide, celebrations should be held. After "Operation Simplification" at Marks & Spencer, Marcus Sieff held a bonfire made up of forms and other paperwork no longer in use.

3. Collect all forms

Gather together all the forms used within your department or organization along with all the procedures and instructions surrounding their use. People are frequently amazed by the number of forms they collect. Estimates of the number of forms used in the organization are usually only about 30 percent of the actual figure. For each form try to calculate the number of pieces of paper that are generated by its use annually.

What are the printing costs for each form? Use the 40:1 rule (costs in use = printing costs x 40) to estimate the annual cost of each form. Produce a list of forms based on cost and focus your attention on redesigning or eliminating the high cost ones. Estimate the total cost of using standard forms in the organization and calculate what the cost savings would be if you achieved your target reduction of 50 percent. The figure you arrive at should provide the motivation to continue.

A recent study in the U.S. found that companies spend $25,000 to print and process the forms in each four-drawer filing cabinet and $2,160 to maintain each cabinet annually. Based on these figures and a reduction of paperwork on a par with Marks & Spencer (1,000 filing cabinets sold off) the cost savings to your company would be close to $6 million a year.

4. Track each form through its life cycle
Chart the life cycle of each form and all of its copies. Who handles it? How long do they spend actually working on it? How long does it spend lying idle waiting to be dealt with or passed on? Are there any major bottlenecks? Talk to the forms users and ask for suggestions as to how the form might be processed more effectively. One insurance company I worked with found that insurance claims took 22 days to process. For the majority of the form's life cycle it was lying untouched on the desks of the six individuals who dealt with a separate part of the form. The total time actually spent writing and reading from the form was only 19 minutes. After a simple reorganization, one person

was given overall responsibility for dealing with the claims, and although the time spent working on each form increased slightly, the average time taken to deal with claims decreased to three days.

5. What is the purpose of each form?

Ask the person or department from which the form originated why that form was introduced. Have circumstances changed dramatically since the form's introduction that render it no longer necessary? Ask those who have to use the form what purpose it serves. Do their answers differ from those given by the form's compilers? If they disagree, investigate further. Could the job be performed effectively if the form was scrapped?

During "Operation Simplification," Marcus Sieff examined the use of the company's stock order forms. These forms had to be filled out by the sales staff every time they spotted that the goods on the shelves were running low. The forms would be processed by the stockroom staff who would bring the goods to the stockroom counter to be collected by the sales staff. In trusting the sales staff to retrieve goods directly from the stockroom, the intervening paperwork was eliminated and goods reached the shelves quicker than ever before.

6. Has means–end inversion occurred?

The correct completion of forms often becomes more important than actually doing the job correctly. Many forms are introduced with the intention of identifying a person doing a job or function incorrectly. However, if the job is not being performed correctly for reasons of poor motivation the introduction of a form will actually make the situation worse. It is always possible to fill out the form correctly and do the job incorrectly.

The distribution staff of one company I worked with had to complete a long checklist for each item that was being delivered to a customer. The checklists were themselves checked to make sure that the correct procedures were being followed. However, the distribution people would use a shortcut method to get the goods on the road and would complete all the checklists at the end of the day. There were problems both with the shortcut method and the checklist method of doing the job. Using the former, the goods would be delivered quickly but occasionally to the wrong location. The latter method meant that the right goods would always go to the right place but the delivery time would be considerably longer. Both methods were leading to customer complaints. Eventually the checklist was abandoned and a simpler method combining suggestions from both management and staff was introduced and performance immediately improved.

7. Evaluate form design

Talk to the form's users. Does filling out the form ever cause stress, anger or confusion because of poor design? Is the layout of the form difficult to follow? Is the key information easy to locate? Is the language in use on the form ambiguous or unintelligible? Take note of the users' suggestions for improved design and incorporate them in a new form. Before any new form is introduced, the form designers should be required to spend at least a day completing the forms themselves in a realistic situation. No new forms should be introduced without significant input from those who will be using it. A trial period of one month should be used for each new form to allow the designers and users to identify any problems. After this time the form can be redesigned, scrapped or left as it is.

8. Can the information be located elsewhere?

Does the form ask for information that can easily be located elsewhere? Could two or more forms that ask for similar types of information be merged? One person in the organization should be given overall responsibility for checking that when new forms are introduced they are not duplicating information requests.

In the U.S., the Paperwork Reduction Act, 1980, legislated for the setting up of a central body to which government agencies could refer to when designing new forms, to see if the information they were looking for existed elsewhere. The Commission on Federal Paperwork had discovered that the six government energy agencies were using almost 220 forms, yielding three and a half million responses annually. Eleven million working hours were required to process these forms but a significant proportion of that time was spent dealing with information that had already been collected and processed by another agency.

9. Form storage

Forms generate huge volumes of paper. Storing this paper can use up the organization's resources unnecessarily. How many forms does your company currently have in storage? Is it essential to keep these forms? Will they be used in the future? Why? What percentage of the forms are actually used? What does it cost the company to store these forms, both before and after use? What would be the worst thing that could happen if you threw out each type of form? Could you live with that event quite comfortably? Draw up a discard schedule for all standard forms and make sure that it is followed.

10. Trial elimination
Each internal form should be considered for a trial elimination. Select a small group of users and ask them to work without the form for a month. This move will meet with great resistance from the bureaucrats, but do it anyway. The users should be aware that the object of the exercise is to identify new and better ways of doing the job. Innovative solutions will never develop from a "but that's the way it has always been done around here" attitude.

ELIMINATING UNNECESSARY MEMOS

There are people here from Salisburys, which we bought ... they sent a memo and they were in the office next door. I went in and said, why don't you come in and tell me what you want to say.

— Gerald Ratner

If we traced a typical memo over its life cycle it might look something like this: A manager decides to implement a paperwork reduction program in her department and decides to use a memo to ask for ideas. The memo is drafted and then redrafted several times to get the wording just right. To encourage her people to pay attention to the memo, the manager marks it as urgent. Each person in the department receives a copy, and as the manager is quite pleased with herself for implementing the paperwork reduction program, she also sends copies to the heads of other departments. The memo soon arrives on desks throughout the organization; it is afforded a quick glance and put aside. No action is taken. Two weeks go by and the manager has only received one reply to her original memo, so she decides to draft a second, as a reminder to others to send her their ideas. Again each person in the department receives a copy and the heads of other departments also have to be kept up to date. The second memo receives a similar response to the first and finally, the issue is brought up at a departmental meeting. It transpires that there is great enthusiasm for the paperwork reduction program; the problem was that people already had so much paperwork on their desks that they didn't have time to respond. The memo had been produced with good intentions but it was an inappropriate mode of communication.

The copies of the memo that were sent to the other departmental heads could be classified as self-serving. Self-congratulation memos are relatively harmless, but the serious problems occur when, because of a lack of trust in the organization, people start to send memos for self-protection. It is ironic that the memo was first introduced to facilitate communication, yet the memo wars that take place in many organizations are symptomatic of a breakdown in communications.

MEMO REDUCTION ACTION PLAN

1. Publicize the memo reduction program
Place an article about the memo program in your company newsletter or launch it dramatically at a company conference or meeting. Enlist the help of the chief executive; if he or she is seen to place a high priority on the reduction of unnecessary

memos, other people in the organization will sit up and take notice.

2. Analyze the memo flow

Either individually, or as part of a group, retrieve all the memos you have filed away. Set aside all those memos which you considered to be irrelevant. This stack will include all those memos written for self-protection, self-importance and self-congratulations. There will also be those memos which were sent with a genuine desire to keep us informed of issues which we don't consider important. What percentage of the memos that land on your desk are irrelevant? Try to calculate the number of unnecessary memos that are sent in your organization every year. Calculate the average number of copies sent, for each memo. What does it cost the organization? Include the time spent producing and reading memos.

3. Obsolete memos

What percentage of the memos that you receive tell you something you already know? Why were they sent? What can you do to prevent these memos from arriving in the future?

4. Identify the memo junkies in the organization

If a significant proportion of the unnecessary memos that land on your desk come from one source, make that person aware of the fact. Both of you will benefit from this: the amount of time that person wastes drafting memos will be reduced and you will no longer have to waste time reading them to find out that they are irrelevant. Impose a strict limit on the number of memos that can be sent by one person in a month.

5. Discard unnecessary memos

Make a big fuss of throwing out all the memos you consider irrelevant. Spread the news around that your department has thrown out 90 percent of all memos kept on file and that in future all unnecessary memos will be discarded. You will find that this will instantly reduce the inflow of memos. Nobody wants to go to the trouble of writing a memo that will be thrown away. You will come up against some resistance to this ruthless attitude but it will mainly come from the memo junkies.

6. What about oral communication?

"We prefer to talk to each other than write to each other," says Sir Allen Sheppard. Tony Burns, the CEO of Ryder Systems, was recently quoted as saying, "The more personally you address the problem the better. You can look someone in the eyes and you can tell by the look in his eyes or the inflection in his voice what the real question or problem is." Gerald Ratner also finds verbal communication to be "more accurate than written communication." Identify the memos that contain information which could have been passed on more quickly and more accurately by word of mouth. Encourage the senders of these memos to talk to you in the future.

7. Beware of electronic mail (E-mail)

E-mail is often seen as the panacea to all memo ills. You will often hear people say that the introduction of E-mail has saved tens of thousands of pieces of paper in their organization, however, this is only one side of the story. In the majority of companies the introduction of E-mail leads to a huge increase in junk memos and correspondingly, a huge increase in the time wasted producing and reading them. The overall effect of E-mail is usually a negative one. The factors that lead to junk memos should be dealt with before electronic transfer of information is introduced in any organization.

8. Eliminate all memos on a trial basis

For a short time period insist that nobody in your department or the company sends a memo. Until you take such drastic action people will not give serious consideration to alternative means of communication. The experiment should last long enough for people to get used to not using memos. Ross Perot, while Chief Executive of General Motors, ran a memoless company. Why should you have any great difficulties doing the same?

9. Memo shortcuts

If it is absolutely essential that information is communicated via a memo, damage-limitation techniques should be employed. Place information memos that need to be read by everyone on a central notice board or send one copy of the memo around the office to be signed and passed on by each person in turn. One company I worked with introduced a tray in which all incoming memos relevant to the department were placed. As people passed by they could glance at the tray to see if it contained anything relevant. The tray is cleared out every Friday evening.

10. Use memos as a last resort

You cannot expect other people to stop sending you memos if there are bits of paper constantly arriving on their desks from you. Resist the temptation to put things in writing when you can walk next door or pick up the telephone to speak to someone.

ELIMINATING UNNECESSARY PROCEDURES

If you are like most office workers in large organizations, everything you do during the day will have a procedure attached to it. Dealing with customers, processing orders, ordering supplies, dealing with your colleagues, are all governed by a series of guidelines. Many of these guidelines are useful but often they serve to prevent things from getting done, to slow things down, to stifle innovation and to assign blame. On top of that, each new procedure that is introduced will lead to a new form or checklist to ensure that it will be carried out correctly.

It might not be appropriate for this book to supply you with a list of procedures to follow to eliminate your own unnecessary procedures. A more direct approach will often work just as well. Buck Rodgers, while at IBM, was constantly receiving complaints from his salespeople about bureaucratic procedures getting in the way of effective performance. Those procedures were contained in what was known as the Branch Office Manuals. Rodgers finally decided that something needed to be done and he flew to the IBM branch office in Salt Lake City. He physically removed the manuals from the shelves and when the managers reacted negatively, predicting chaos, he simply told them to use their common sense. Within 90 days the branch office manuals had been rewritten and reduced by 75 percent. More importantly, huge volumes of paperwork that had accompanied the old procedures were eliminated.

If you agree with the sentiment behind Rodgers's method, but consider it too ruthless, look at what happened at Nordstrom, the U.S. retailing giant. They threw out a several thousand-page procedure manuals and replaced it with one sentence, "Use your own best judgement at all times." That is ruthless!

HOW TO REDUCE THE TIME YOU SPEND ON OTHER PEOPLE'S PAPERWORK

Throughout the day we face a steady stream of people heading towards our desk with paperwork for our attention. While some of this paperwork is essential if we are to do our job well, a large part of it is unnecessary and should remain on the desks of our colleagues. The Clear Your Desk! survey found that we face an average of eight unwanted paperwork interruptions a day. We can therefore expect to receive about 40 unwanted items every week. If we dealt with every unwanted item and each one took an hour to complete, there would be no time left for anything else.

If you allow others to dump paperwork on your desk and put all your effort into clearing their backlog of work, very soon you will find yourself running out of time while the people around you begin to run out of work. I have often sat in offices and heard people exclaim, "But there is nothing I can do about it." Then in the next sentence they are saying to others around them, "Send me some information on it"; "You will need to put it in writing"; "Send a memo"; "Write me a report"; "Send me a draft before it goes out" and so on, encouraging others to add to their backlog of paperwork. It is your own management style that contributes more than anything to the inflow of unnecessary paper. Do you recognize any of the following scenarios?

"It looks urgent, I'll get to it right away"
A colleague rushes into your office waving an "urgent" fax. "We've got a real problem on our hands." Without thinking you have grabbed the fax and become immersed in the problem. We too often get involved unnecessarily in crisis paperwork. What appears to be

urgent is not always important and should not therefore be given our attention. The rush of adrenalin that accompanies the handling of a crisis is difficult to resist. Many people like to see themselves as troubleshooters and actively encourage others to pass on their crises. The danger in dealing with urgent paperwork is that very often the pay-off is quite low. Ignore the word "urgent" in future and ask yourself what the pay-off will be from all incoming paperwork. Even if the crisis is genuine, whose crisis is it? Why has the person who is bringing the problem to your attention not already dealt with it? Can you delegate the handling of the crisis to people around you? One manager I know has a sign on the door of his office which says "The lack of planning on your part does not constitute a crisis on my part." He gets very few people rushing into his office with urgent paperwork.

"I'm the best person for the job"
Paperwork that should be tackled by one of your colleagues often ends up on your desk because you believe that you are the best person for the job. Many managers that have been newly promoted spend a disproportionate amount of their time on paperwork that was important in their previous position. The sales manager writes proposals for his junior salespeople and the accountant promoted to managing director continues to deal with much of the financial paperwork. They can almost certainly do the job better than anyone else, otherwise they would not have been promoted. Tackling the paperwork you feel comfortable with will mean that the high pay-off items associated with your new job will be left unfinished and build up on your desk. What unnecessary paperwork will typically arrive on your desk because you like dealing with it? Who would tackle it if you were not around? Let them deal with it in future.

Even if they can't do the job as well as you now, they can learn. Meanwhile you can concentrate on your high pay-off paperwork.

"They are not capable of doing it by themselves"
The less you trust people around you to do their jobs well, the greater the amount of paperwork that will land on your desk. Documents will constantly be arriving on the desk for your approval, your authorization, your input and your analysis. It is time to give the people around you greater responsibility. Don't make a habit of looking over their shoulder at every stage of a project expecting something to go wrong. A dependency relationship will develop whereby at the first sign of a problem your staff will come rushing to you, paperwork in hand. If mistakes are made don't punish the people involved but encourage them to learn from the experience. If your colleagues come up against a problem ask them to try and find a solution first and to come to you only as a last resort. If your desk is cluttered with documents that require your signature before they can be processed, increase the authorization levels of those around you to cut out the paperwork or delegate the authorization.

"Leave it with me"
You are working at your desk when a colleague carrying a report interrupts you with: "I have a problem with the XYZ project." You are too busy trying to catch up on yesterday's backlog of paperwork to give the matter your full attention. You look up and instead of saying what you mean, "Go away," the words "Leave it with me" come out. The paperwork lands on your desk and the problem has been solved in the short term. However, you have now taken on responsibility for moving the

paperwork on to the next stage. Later on in the day your colleague will arrive back in the office to see if you have dealt with his paperwork. The more you ask people to leave paperwork on your desk, the greater will be the line of colleagues outside your office waiting impatiently for you to finish their work.

At no time when you are helping someone else with a problem should their problem become your problem. If you face an unwanted interruption for a colleague wishing to discuss a paperwork problem explain that you are busy and arrange a convenient time to discuss it. You will often find that the problem will be solved before you meet to discuss it without you having to get involved. When colleagues rush into your office waving paperwork, rather than grabbing it say, "Tell me what the real problem is here," and then ask, "What do you think should be done?" When they have given you their answer ask them to go and do it.

"Leave it with me!"

"I don't want to cause offense"
This rationalization for allowing others to dump paperwork on your desk is common. "Well if someone

has taken the trouble to bring paperwork into my office, then I owe it to them to give it my attention." The real offense here is of course being caused by those arriving with unnecessary paperwork and yet you will hear yourself thanking them for it: "Oh yes, that looks interesting, thanks a lot." This sends out the message that you appreciate people leaving things on the desk and will encourage more of the same behavior in the future. It pays to be ruthless occasionally. The famous story of a junior executive who sent his boss a rather loquacious memo serves to illustrate appropriate ruthlessness. The following day an envelope landed on the junior executive's desk containing the memo, which had been put through the shredder. The message was quite clear, "Don't waste my time." This story rapidly spread throughout the organization and did more to reduce the flow of memos than any committee spending a year on the task could have done. You should also be proactive about letting people know what incoming paperwork you do not want arriving on your desk.

"I need to have an open door policy"
Many managers like to be seen as accessible to their staff and as a result do nothing to stop the inflow of unnecessary paperwork. The "open door" policy is a laudable one but should only be used in conjunction with a "clear desk" policy. The open door can just as easily accommodate people walking out with paperwork as it can them coming in with that paperwork. Make it clear to your colleagues that you will not allow your accessibility to be abused. There is only a certain amount of paperwork that you can deal with in any one day and they should be made aware of that fact. Unless paperwork is important it should be kept outside your office. The best form of open door policy is to walk through it and engage in

"managing by wandering around." Get out and talk to people and preclude the need for them to come to you.

COPING WITH A PAPERHOLIC BOSS

Each year the Clear Your Desk! Organization launches a search to find the most cluttered desk in Britain. At least 70 percent of the nominations come from people who are complaining about the cluttered desk of their boss. Whether you are a secretary or a senior manager, if your boss works from a cluttered desk you will suffer because of it.

Stacks of paper may land on your desk for no other reason than the fact that there is no more space left on the desk of your boss. Documents that your boss should have discarded will be passed on for your attention. The paperwork that is correctly delegated arrives without any clear instructions and as a result it hibernates on your desk because you are not sure how or when to tackle it. You will also find yourself wasting time dealing with paperwork that should have landed on someone else's desk while at the same time they are staring blankly at paperwork that should have come to you.

Your boss will constantly lose things on the desk. You will frequently be asked for documents that you know are lying on the boss's desk but he or she has just spent 20 minutes looking for them there and is convinced that you have them. Even worse are the occasions when your boss is away from the office and you have to spend half an hour trying to locate some "urgent" paperwork on his or her desk. The mountain of unfinished paperwork will also lead to an unnecessarily large number of crises, many of which will land on your desk to be dealt with.

The paperholic boss

COPING WITH A PAPERHOLIC BOSS ACTION PLAN

1. Get your boss to clear his or her desk
It will not be easy because like most addicts paperholic bosses will refuse to admit that they have a problem. They will undoubtedly have all the excuses discussed in Chapter 1 at their fingertips: "But I know where everything is" and "I'm a creative person." Be persistent and enlist the help of other people in the office.

2. Present your boss with a copy of this book
Better still, send him or her to a Clear Your Desk! seminar.

3. Point out to your boss the negative effects of the clutter as they occur
Every time you spot the frantic searching with head stuck in the in-tray trying to locate items remind your boss that it wouldn't be as much trouble if he or she worked from a clear desk. Be

careful to be good humored about it. Take a blank piece of paper and write on it "Each piece of paper you have on the desk will distract you up to five times a day." Place the piece of paper on your boss's desk where it will be noticed (at least five times a day!) and will reinforce the message. People who have tried this with their boss report that it works extremely well.

4. Ensure that you regularly review your priorities with your boss

Decide with your boss what your high pay-off paperwork is and identify together the time-wasting paperwork that normally arrives on your desk from his or hers. Discuss ways in which this unnecessary inflow can be reduced or eliminated.

5. Ask your boss to accompany all delegated paper-work with clear instructions either written or oral

Rather than allowing your boss to tell you that everything is urgent, agree on a realistic deadline for completion of the paperwork. This is especially important if you are working for more than one boss.

6. Agree with your boss about a level of performance that is acceptable when dealing with different types of paperwork

When gathering information for a report, it is better to send it 95 percent complete rather than spend hours searching out that last 5 percent that will make little overall difference to the report. It is better to send an internal memo containing spelling errors rather than wasting time retyping it.

7. If you can, try to reduce the amount of paper that lands on the desk of your boss

A large portion of this will find its way onto your

desk. Filter out the unnecessary paperwork before your boss sees it, including junk mail, low pay-off reports and memos and all the non-urgent, non-important paperwork.

8. Keep an eye on the unfinished paperwork on the desk of your boss

As important deadlines approach remind your boss by saying things like, "We should keep the meeting short because I know you need to finish the XYZ project by tomorrow evening." Your boss will agree but in reality you have just reminded him or her to extract the paperwork from the bottom of the in-tray and deal with it.

9. Encourage your boss to plan more considerately

If you work a lot of overtime because your boss dumps urgent paperwork on your desk at 5:00 P.M. just as you are about to go home, encourage your boss to use a prioritized to-do list and to work on the important paperwork before lunch. Your boss will waste less time during the day dealing with low pay-off paperwork, and the letter that has to go out in today's mail might arrive on your desk to be typed at 11:50 A.M. rather than 4:50 P.M.

10. Use tactfully chosen signs

Place a "No Dumping" or "Clutter Free Zone" sign close to your desk to get the message across to your boss in a good humored way.

REDUCING THE INFLOW OF PAPERWORK FROM OUTSIDE THE ORGANIZATION

If every morning sees your desk besieged by an avalanche of mail, you may find it useful to put some of the techniques in this section into practice.

The Clear Your Desk! survey showed that 30 percent of the letters that land on the desk can be classified as junk mail. In the U.S., every adult receives about 500 items of junk mail each year. In the U.K. we only receive about 10 percent of that figure but we are catching up rapidly. "My junk mail always goes straight in the trash," cries the streetwise manager, but it doesn't. We waste time opening and reading it and it often remains on the desk for weeks distracting us before being consigned to the trash. How much unsolicited mail is currently lying on your desk? You will often hear others complain about the amount of junk mail they receive and they will point to a stack of items they have hoarded on the desk. The most effective way of dealing with junk mail is to stop it being sent in the first place.

"Send me some information!"

Stop asking people to send you information that you do not want. When you pick up the telephone to hear, "Hello my name is X from the ABC company and I would like to tell you about the services we provide ..." how do you get rid of this person? Have you ever heard yourself saying, "Send me some information?" It is the knee-jerk reaction that occurs every time we hear a telesalesperson at the other end of the telephone line. We have no intention of dealing with that company but we waste both their time and ours by inviting them to put something in the mail. If you cannot have your calls screened there are alternative ways of saying no. "I am in the middle of a meeting at the moment, but I don't think I am interested anyway" or "We have just got one, so we are both wasting our time talking to each other."

If you are receiving regular mailings from certain companies that you do not want to do business with, telephone them and ask to be taken off their database.

If you are dealing with several potential suppliers and finally choose one, telephone the rest thanking them for their efforts and ask them not to send you any further information.

Do not allow your receptionist to give out individual names at the switchboard. Receptionists are continually receiving calls from individuals who want to know who is in charge of photocopiers, recruitment and stationery. Companies who have introduced the no names policy report a 70 percent reduction in junk mail in the first year.

Depending on the type of organization in which you work, there are other techniques you can use to cut down incoming mail. If you receive a large number of orders through the mail you might consider introducing a telephone ordering service for your clients. You could also encourage potential clients to call rather than write by just including your telephone number in advertisements.

ELIMINATING SELF-GENERATED CHAOS

Once you have eliminated the unnecessary paperwork that others place on your desk it is time to overcome your worst enemy, yourself. We all use memo pads, message slips, Post-it™ notes and other blank pieces of paper to keep track of commitments, to draft letters, to take notes at meetings, to jot down ideas, to record details of telephone conversations and to plan projects. At the end of a busy day these bits of paper have proliferated into a mountain of self-generated chaos on the desk. Most of the information on these pieces of paper can be classified as necessary but what is unnecessary is the way the information is scattered around the desk. The chaos can only result in more time spent trying to locate information, unwanted distractions and missed opportunities.

To keep control of your personal paperwork on the desk you need to follow three simple guidelines:

1. Keep loose pieces of paper off the desk.
Throw out your notepads, Post-it™ notes, message slips and other blank pieces of paper. As long as there are scraps of paper on the desk the temptation is to use them. If the telephone rings and you need to take down some details, the natural reaction is to grab the nearest piece of paper.

2. Develop a personal organization system that suits you.
Mark McCormack, the sports management guru and author of *What They Don't Teach You at Harvard Business School* (Harper Collins, 1984), has stated that he does not know a single successful executive who does not have some kind of personal organization system. The most effective way of organizing your personal paperwork is to keep everything in one place, in a good personal organizer.

Your commitments, activities and to-do items should all be kept together on a to-do list rather than scattered around the desk on a series of Post-it™ notes.

Each project you have undertaken should have an overview page outlining each stage of the project and other relevant information. Before each meeting you should write down any ideas you have on a page set aside for that purpose. Decisions made during that meeting should be placed on the same page. Most office workers have a personal organizer but very few use it effectively. The key is to tailor the organizer to the way you work, develop a system that suits you and stick to it, religiously.

3. Write everything down.

You cannot hope to keep track of all the information that passes across your desk by storing it in your head. Richard Branson carries with him, 24 hours a day, a large red, bound notebook. In it he notes details of every conversation, every meeting, every telephone call and every idea he has. In his office there are a series of these red notebooks going back over 20 years. Mark McCormack uses a very effective system for keeping track of his communications. He calls it his "talk to" system. He carries in his jacket pocket a series of index cards, one for each of his key clients and executives. Every time he thinks of something he wants to talk to someone about he writes it down on that person's card. This simple system can be used in conjunction with a personal organizer by having a page for every person on which you would plan and record all communications. Professor George Bain uses a simple system to keep track of commitments made to him by others:

I have a nag book in my top left hand drawer. When I have a meeting I always like to have an outcome and I say, "What's going to happen here?" and they might say, "George I have to do a paper for you on

*this" and I say, "Great when will you have it ready"
and they say, "The 14th of November" and I
usually ostentatiously make a display of writing it
down. They know that on the 14th November my
secretary will be on the phone saying, "George is
wondering why he hasn't got the paper."*

CHAPTER FOUR

Paperwork: The Four Choices

Be absolutely ruthless with paperwork and be prepared to throw quite a bit of it away. Be selective about what you keep as current action.

— Sir Allen Sheppard

FROM THE MOMENT we arrive in the office each morning we are faced with a steady stream of documents landing on our desks: letters, faxes, computer printouts, message slips, files, magazines, memos and brochures. Most of us will deal with somewhere between 20 and 50 pieces of incoming paperwork every day. In the last chapter we looked at some of the techniques we can use to reduce the inflow of unnecessary paper. But, however successful we are in putting those techniques into practice, we still have to deal effectively with the paperwork that does arrive, important or otherwise. Failure to deal with each piece of paper as it lands on the desk will lead to a rapid build up of clutter and the distractions, long searches, missed opportunities and the inevitable stress that accompanies it.

Nothing short of ruthlessness will allow you to keep control of the paperwork that lands on your desk. Lew Wasserman, president of MCA, was renowned for being ruthless, both with his own paperwork and that of his executives. He would wander through the company's offices late in the evening looking for paper on the desks of others. Anything he found would be thrown straight into the trash. He worked on the principle that if you can't get work done before you leave at the end of the day then it is not worth doing. His tactics reportedly resulted in huge increases of productivity.

However, before you start waging war on other people's paperwork, ensure that your own desk is under control. If you want to encourage those around you to adopt a clear desk policy, then tell them why—it is to make their jobs easier to perform. Poorly implemented clear desk policies can rapidly backfire as the clear desk becomes an end in itself, rather than a means to an end. Sir John Harvey-Jones recalls walking into Marks & Spencer around the time of "Operation Simplification": there were two executives sitting at their desks with no paperwork whatsoever around them. On inquiring about this, Sir John was told how Simon Marks, the chairman, would tear up any piece of paper he found lying on anybody's desk. When Sir John asked for the document he had come to collect one of the executives suddenly disappeared under his desk and started to shuffle around a pile of papers he had on the floor, hidden from view. The document was eventually re-trieved. This unfortunate reaction to the clear desk policy appears to have spread throughout the company. A short while later the internal mailman came into the office to deliver the morning mail. Instead of placing the letters on the desk, or in a tray, the elderly gentleman stooped down and slipped the letters underneath the desk.

You may choose to use the above method to keep your desktop clear of paper, though I wouldn't recommend it. There is a more practical and effective alternative. It involves following two simple rules. The first is to deal with each item of paperwork as soon as possible after it lands on your desk. The second is to make one of four decisions about each item of paperwork:

- Should I act on it?
- Should I pass it on to someone else's desk?
- Does it belong in my filing system?
- Should I throw it away?

Rule 1: Deal with each piece of paper as soon as it lands on the desk!

There is no easier way to deal with paperwork than to leave it on your desktop, untouched. Equally, there is no less effective way of dealing with it. If you pick up every piece of paper as soon as it lands on your desk, and place it somewhere else, there will be nothing to distract your attention away from your current project. It is as simple as that. You don't necessarily have to stop work every time a new document arrives. Wait until you have finished what you are doing and then deal with it. It is a good idea to keep your in-tray off the desk and behind you, if possible, so you won't be distracted by incoming documents. Richard Branson advises, "Don't let paperwork sit and drag, act on it almost as soon as you see it." Gerald Ratner would have a better excuse than most to allow paperwork to build up on his desk. He runs Britain's biggest High Street jewellers from what must be Britain's biggest desk. He sits at a 20 square foot, leather covered oak giant. However, he deals with paperwork as soon as it arrives, and warns others, "Don't

Don't let paperwork sit and drag

put it off, deal with it straight away, because then it mounts up." If you are far away from your desk for any length of time, as soon as you get back decide what to do with each item of paperwork that has been placed on your desk in your absence.

Handle each piece of paper only once
This is one of the golden rules of effective paper handling. Most of us pick up a piece of paper and put it back down on the desk to be dealt with later. Not only does this add to the clutter, it also means that the next time we pick it up we have to familiarize ourselves with it all over again. You should only need to look at a piece of paper once to decide that either it belongs in the trash or that it requires immediate action.

If you need to pass paperwork on to someone else you should write instructions for them on the piece of paper the first time you see it, rather than putting it aside and dealing with it later. Paperwork that belongs in your filing system should not be placed in a file stack and then filed away. If your filing system is well organized you will have no problem filing it straight away. There are exceptions to any rule and in some cases it may be more appropriate to deal with paperwork at a later date. Keep it off the desk until then.

Work on one project at a time
The essence of the clear desk policy is that you restrict your workspace to one project at a time. The desk may be covered with reports, computer printouts, letters, memo pads and other items of paperwork, but if they are all related to the same project then you are working effectively. Every time you have finished working on one project you should clear the paperwork from your desk—not into the nearest drawer to be sorted out later

but into an appropriate file or space. If someone walks into your office with a piece of paper and sits down for a few minutes to discuss it with you, there is no need to go to the trouble of filing the paperwork away. However, if you have scheduled a meeting at your desk, then it should be cleared of paperwork before you start.

How to handle paper interruptions
The Clear Your Desk! survey showed that office workers faced an average of eight unwanted paperwork interruptions a day. All too often we end up dealing with the interrupting paperwork in preference to the more important paperwork we have in front of us. In the chaotic world of most offices the words "urgent" and "important" are frequently confused. There is, however, an important distinction. Urgent paperwork means that there is a tight deadline associated with the item. Important paperwork means that dealing with the item will result in a high pay-off. What is urgent is not always important and what is important is not always urgent. The first question we should ask ourselves when facing a paperwork interruption is, "What will the pay-off be?" And the second question we should ask is, "When should I deal with it?" The model below should help you to deal with interruptions effectively.

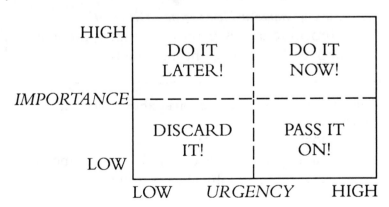

High importance and high urgency: Do it now!
An advertising executive is interrupted by one of her creative colleagues who has just completed the final advertising copy for a new campaign. The presentation to the client is later that afternoon so she files away the research reports she has been studying and concentrates on evaluating the new copy.

High importance and low urgency: Do it later!
A colleague walks into the office with a letter from a potential client inviting the agency to pitch for the launch of a major new product. The deadline is several weeks away so she files the letter and arranges a meeting for the following week to discuss what tactics they will employ.

Low importance and high urgency: Pass it on!
An urgent fax arrives from a client seeking to clarify some minor details for a press reception in only three hours. Getting involved would be a real time stealer so the response is delegated to a junior colleague who is familiar with the account.

Low importance and low urgency: Discard it!
A brochure arrives on the desk from a potential supplier. It goes straight into the trash.

Rule 2: Make one of four choices about each piece of paper.
Since paper was invented in 105 B.C. there have only been four things people could do with paperwork. Whether you are a Sir John Harvey-Jones who works for

33 different organizations or an office junior at your first desk, there are still only four things you can do with a piece of paper that lands on your desk. You can *act on it, pass it on* to someone else, *file it away* or *place it in the trash*.

Act-on *Pass-on*

File *Discard*

The effective paper handling habit
Habits, both good and bad, are formed as a result of repeating an action hundreds of times. Coming to work each morning, we do not consciously have to decide which route to take or to stop and think which floor our office is on: our unconscious mind takes over and we react according to habit. In the same way, every time we pick up a piece of paper from the desk and put it back down again without making a definite decision on what to do with it, we are reacting unconsciously. This indecision habit has developed over a number of years and through dealing with thousands of pieces of paper in a similar manner.

Breaking this old habit and substituting more productive paper handling behavior in its place, will neither be a quick nor an easy process. Each time a piece of paper lands on the desk we must make a conscious decision about what to do with it. Should we act on it, should we pass it on, should we file it or should we place it in the trash? If we deal with 20 items of incoming paperwork a day, then we should ask ourselves these questions 20 times a day. If 80 items arrive for our attention, then we must go through the decision process 80 times. Each report, memo, letter, message slip and fax that we pick up should be put through the decision process until finally it becomes a habit, and stopping to ask ourselves these questions can be delegated to the unconscious.

Act-on paperwork

Much of the paperwork that arrives on the desk is in the form of a direct instruction or a request for further action. However, there is a big gap between knowing that action is required and actually performing that action. If the newly arrived paperwork is difficult, boring or uncomfortable, despite knowing we should "Do it now!," we will use all our ingenuity to avoid "doing it." We may spot something that we know should really be tackled without delay, but which we just don't feel like doing. It might be a letter which needs a reply, a report we have to write or a memo requesting action. The piece of paper is pushed aside. At the same time a little voice inside our head is saying, "I'm too busy to tackle it right now"; "It's not that urgent"; "It's not due yet and anyway I work better under pressure"; "It's too early, I'll do it later"; "It's too late, I'll do it tomorrow"; "I just don't know where to start"; "Some-one else will tackle it"; "We've missed the deadline on it by now." We practice these excuses hour after hour, day after day, until eventually we actually believe them to be true. And as we push the uncomfortable paperwork aside we immerse ourselves in the quick, the easy, the fun, the comfortable paperwork of which there is an abundance on the desk.

This habit of procrastination is more difficult to maintain while working from a clear desk. There are fewer places to hide the paperwork we are trying to put off. Also absent will be the mountains of low pay-off, time-filling paperwork that we use to ease our consciences while we are procrastinating.

As the "act-on" paperwork steadily builds up on our desks, we begin to miss deadlines and opportunities. We find ourselves facing more and more crises as a result of our inaction, and every evening as we leave the office we promise ourselves that tomorrow we will get it done. Sir Allen Sheppard warns, "ensure that you never get behind with paperwork because once you do, hell and all breaks loose." The speed with which Sir John Harvey-Jones tackles his paperwork can be matched by very few, "I like to get the day's paperwork finished by 9:00 A.M. if I possibly can."

It is of course sometimes appropriate to delay action on paperwork. We may need to wait until we have collected further information on the subject, we may need to consult with a colleague before making a decision, the paperwork may result in a lower pay-off than several items currently on our "to do" list or the deadline may be some time away. "Do it later" paper-work presents us with a dilemma; where should it be kept until we act on it? The usual choice is to leave the paperwork on the desk, "to remind me to do it later," because we fear that if the paperwork is filed away it will be forgotten about. Even if the required action is a month away we feel more comfortable leaving the paperwork on the desk with the unfortunate result that when the time comes for action it is well and truly buried on the desk and the deadline passes without our noticing.

Keeping control of your "do it later" paperwork involves three simple steps:

1. Decide when you are going to tackle the paperwork. Some items will determine their own deadlines: you might have to read a report for a meeting in three weeks' time. Other items may not be so clear cut: you may be waiting for someone to get back to you before proceeding further or you have decided to deal with an item, if you have the time. You should still choose a date on which you will check the progress of these items. On that date they should again be put through the decision process, should I act-on ... should I discard? Failure to do this will result in a large backlog of "someday" paperwork.

2. Make a definite commitment to deal with the paperwork on the chosen date by writing it down on the relevant page in your diary.

3. Place the paperwork in the appropriate action file. The four most useful categories of action file are: correspondence, meetings, reading and projects. Some people, including Sir John Harvey-Jones, use a bring forward file to keep track of paperwork of this type. Special action files can also be set up for particular projects. Your action files should be located in a desk drawer or another easily accessible place. Their use will be discussed in more detail in Chapter 6.

You will find that the top executives clear their "do it later" paperwork from the desk and keep it in a special place. Sir Allen Sheppard carries all his paperwork in a big case. "So I know when I'm getting behind with paperwork, because I have to carry two cases." Gerald Ratner has a special drawer in his desk for holding paperwork of this type.

Pass-on paperwork
Paperwork should be passed on to the desk of someone else, either if it has been misrouted to your desk or if you decide to delegate it. In either case the paperwork should not be on your desk for a second longer than is necessary. If you are about to delegate paperwork, decide who the best person for the job is. Try to avoid delegating projects to paperholics; you will receive numerous memos on how the project is proceeding, any reports produced will be twice as long as necessary and the delegatee will constantly interrupt you with paperwork problems. With paperholics around you, delegating can be more trouble than it's worth.

It is essential to make sure that the delegation instructions are clear, whether they are written or verbal, to ensure that paperwork is not lying untouched on someone else's desk because they are not sure what you want them to do with it. Alternatively, they may put too much effort into the job, producing a full blown report instead of a few brief details you required. Always set a deadline with the delegatee and make a note of it on the relevant page in your diary.

Gerald Ratner advises, "In business there is no need to get bogged down in paperwork, you can always delegate it." You should delegate as much of your routine, low pay-off paperwork as possible but try to avoid the trap of delegating what should have been discarded. Also delegate important paperwork to those around you as this will encourage your colleagues to make decisions on their own.

File paperwork

Filing paperwork away should be a relatively straightforward procedure, but this is not usually the case as we do make life difficult for ourselves. Stacks of paper we should have filed constantly pile up on our desks, shelves and floors. At best we have a "to file" tray on the desk, but it is only cleared when its contents have toppled over several times. We seem to be constantly searching for paperwork among stacks on the desk that should have been filed.

Why does the simple process of placing a piece of paper in a drawer beside our desk present us with so many problems? One of the reasons is the fact that our filing systems are so disorganized. The sheer mental effort required to decide where to file something means that we take the easy option and leave paperwork on the desk. The fear that filing items in that disorganized mess of a filing system will mean losing them forever is also a very powerful motivator to hoard things on the desk.

If you follow the guidelines in Chapter 6 for reorganizing your filing system, the process of putting paperwork away will be much less troublesome. Get into the habit of filing paperwork away as soon as you have finished dealing with it. If you encounter a large amount of incoming paperwork that requires filing, use a file tray, to temporarily capture it and file in batches. The file tray, however, should never be left on the desk as it will become a resting place for all your other paperwork as well. Place it on top of the filing cabinet or in some other appropriate location.

Discard paperwork

Most of the paperwork that arrives on the desk will eventually be discarded, but it causes an awful lot of trouble before that happens. Eighty five percent of the paperwork that we choose to file rather than discard is never looked at again. The solution lies in knowing which paperwork we will never use again and in being ruthless enough to dump unnecessary paperwork. "Throw away anything that is unnecessary immediately. Anything that arrives on the desk that you don't need, put it in the trash, it's one of the most important things to have in business," is the advice from Gerald Ratner. We are all aware that junk belongs in the trash, but few of us are effective at putting it there, and very often our definition of junk is far too narrow. Sir John Harvey-Jones is another preacher of the discard message: "My main filing aid is a waste paper basket. I have a sort of basket in my office."

PAPERWORK DIARY: THE *ACT-ON, PASS-ON, FILE, DISCARD* PROCESS IN ACTION

Maria is a manager in a large corporation who works from a clear desk. The activities in the diary below show how she handles paperwork effectively.

9:00 A.M. In the morning mail there is an inquiry from a potentially lucrative client. Maria decides to send a reply that afternoon and she jots down a reminder in her diary to tackle the project. She places the letter in her correspondence action file which she always has on her desk when going through the mail. (Act-on—correspondence action file.)

9:05 A.M.   There is a letter from a client querying an invoice. Maria places it in her out-tray to be passed on to the accounts department. (Pass-on.)

9:50 A.M.   Maria's secretary places an agenda on her desk which is for a meeting in two weeks time. Maria places the paperwork in her meeting action file and puts a reminder in her diary two days before the meeting to review the agenda. (Act-on—meeting action file.)

10:40 A.M.   A fax arrives. Maria continues working on an important report for another 20 minutes until she has completed it. She then reviews the fax and decides to act on it straight away. (Act-on—now.)

11:20 A.M.   A brochure is left on the desk outlining a supplier's new price list. Maria has already received a memo on the subject so the brochure is placed in the trash. (Discard.)

12:05 P.M.   A long-winded report lands on the desk. Maria decides to ask someone else to read the report and to provide a verbal summary. She writes instructions on the cover of the report: how long the summary should last and a deadline. She then makes a note in her diary of the deadline. (Pass-on—delegate.)

2:50 P.M. A colleague comes in to show her an interesting magazine article. Maria decides the article is worth reading but not straight away, so she makes a photocopy of the article and places it in her reading file. (Act-on—reading file.)

3:20 P.M. Maria's secretary brings in a proof of a recruitment advertisement. It is not an urgent matter and she wants to get the input of the managing director. She makes a note in her diary to deal with it the next day and places the advertisement in her projects action file. (Act-on—projects file.)

3:50 P.M. While Maria is out of the office at a meeting, a colleague returns a borrowed report. Maria spots it immediately on her return and files it in the correct folder in her filing cabinet. (File.)

CHAPTER FIVE

Priority Paperwork

Richard Branson's priority paperwork: Information regarding Virgin Atlantic Airways and the regulatory authorities, letters, memos and reports concerning the Civil Aviation Authority, Department of Transport, British Airports Authority or competitors. He places a very high priority on passenger complaints and he always likes to respond to them personally if possible. There is a visitors book on Virgin Airways which goes to every first-class passenger and they give their comments on the flight. Richard likes to see these every month, which is a form of direct quality control.

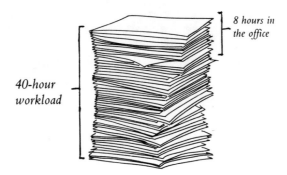

8 hours in
the office

40-hour
workload

SO FAR WE have looked at techniques for reducing the amount of unnecessary paper that lands on the desk and for dealing effectively with the paperwork that does arrive. Put these techniques into practice and you will have mastered the basic skills of effective paper handling. The aim of this chapter is to help you to develop further those skills and to give you complete mastery over your paper workload. By evaluating the pay-off from each piece of paper that lands on the desk, you can fine-tune the effectiveness of the act-on, pass-on, file, discard decision process. If the expected pay-off from an item of incoming paperwork is high we should act on it ourselves rather than pass it on or discard it. In deciding whether or not to file an item we should evaluate what the future pay-off will be; if it is negligible, then the item should be discarded.

HOW EFFECTIVELY DO YOU HANDLE YOUR PRIORITY PAPERWORK?

The questionnaire below will help you to evaluate how you deal with your paperwork priorities. When dealing with each question do not answer it according to what you think you should do, but according to what you actually do. Place a check in the box for each time you answer "yes."

1. If asked to find the three items of paper-work on your desk which would lead

to the highest pay-off, would you have to search for them in different stacks of paper? ☐

2. Do you often plan to tackle certain items of paperwork on the desk but fail to do so because you have been too busy coping with incoming paperwork? ☐

3. In dealing with your backlog of paperwork do you work through the stack of papers on your desk from the top down, picking out items which need attention? ☐

4. When faced with uncomfortable paperwork do you ever find yourself dealing with lower pay-off, but more interesting items first? ☐

5. Does a piece of paper catching your attention out of the corner of your eye often determine which item you deal with next? ☐

6. When you are not at your desk do items of unfinished paperwork often spring into your conscious mind to remind you to deal with them the next time you are back in the office? ☐

7. Have you given up using to-do lists because they are more trouble than they are worth? ☐

8. Do you often stay late in the office or bring work home to try and catch up

on the backlog of paperwork? ☐

9. Do you find that your job is too reactive for to-do lists? ☐

10. If your working day was restricted to two hours could you produce a list, without hesitating, of the paperwork you would need to get done? ☐

If you have placed checks in five or more boxes then you are probably spending too much time dealing with pay-off paperwork that lands on your desk. If you have checked all ten boxes, your desk is probably crammed with high pay-off paperwork that has not been dealt with yet. The next time you set foot in your office close the door and do nothing else until the backlog of important paperwork has been cleared from the desk. If you have checked only one or two boxes, read this chapter carefully and then ask yourself the questions a second time.

As office workers, we hoard an average of 40 hours of unfinished paperwork on the desk demanding our attention. If we sat down at the desk on Monday morning and set a target of working through the backlog of paperwork and clearing it by Friday evening, 40 work hours away, we wouldn't even come close to achieving this target. Although we spend 40 hours a week or so in the office, a large proportion of that time is taken up with meetings and informal communications with others. Then we have to deal with the unwanted interruptions and crises. The Clear Your Desk! survey shows that we spend five and a half hours a week fire-fighting. Add to that the time we waste desperately trying to locate documents on or around the desk, and already about two-thirds of our time is committed. In the remaining time we must also deal with the inflow of new documents onto the desk, which never seems to stop. Friday evening comes and the mountain of paperwork on the desk is just as high. We have managed to clear five or six hours of work from the top, but it has been replaced by new documents.

What can we do? There are two ways of attempting to get the paperwork mountain under control. The first, a course of action chosen by most of us is to spend more time in the office to try and catch up and then to cram documents into our already bulging briefcases to tackle at home. However, the longer we work the less productive we are, and we can all testify to falling asleep in front of the TV set or in bed with a report in one hand and a pen in the other. The other course of action is one in which we are all experts but which we never put into practice, prioritizing our workload. We can never hope to deal with all the paperwork that lands on our desk. The key to dealing with paperwork successfully is to aim for the maximum pay-off from the time we spend working on it.

$25,000 ADVICE

In the 1930's, Charles Schwab was the president of Bethlehem Steel, a U.S. company. Although a very successful executive, he believed that he was not as productive as he might be. As a result he called in one of the time management gurus of the day, a man called Ivy Lee. Mr. Lee followed him around for two weeks making a note of everything he said, everything he did and every piece of paper he tackled. At the end of the two weeks he sat in Charles Schwab's office and handed him a piece of paper. On it were written three pieces of advice:

1. Make a list of things to-do every day.
2. Prioritize the activities on that list.
3. Tackle the activities in order of decreasing pay-off.

Charles Schwab was initially taken aback. He was accustomed to receiving 100-page reports from people who were trying to hide the fact that they didn't know what they were talking about. Confused, he asked Ivy Lee what he expected to be paid for such succinct advice. The reply was to put the three principles into practice for one month and then to pay Ivy Lee what he thought the advice was worth. One month later a piece of paper landed on Ivy's desk. It was a check for $25,000. Charles Schwab was later quoted as saying that it was the best business advice he had ever received and it had helped him to build Bethlehem Steel into the largest independent steel producer in the world.

The advice given to Charles Schwab is as valuable today as it was in the 1930's. We can apply the Lee principles directly to the management of our paper workload. Always use a to-do list to keep track of your outstanding paperwork, prioritize the paperwork on that list, and in deciding what item to deal with next, choose the one that will lead to the highest pay-off. Putting the principles into practice is a three step process.

Step 1: Keep track of all your paperwork commitments and activities by using a to-do list every day.
What happens when we don't use to-do lists?

Each time we glance at an item of incoming paperwork and place it on top of the nearest stack having decided we will "do it later," we write a mental message slip to ourselves as a reminder to deal with it. This message slip is stored in our unconscious mind in the hope that it will resurface into our consciousness at the right time and the activity will be completed. The more unfinished pieces of paper we leave on the desk, the greater the number of mental message slips that are produced, cluttering our minds, nagging us to get things done. How many unfinished paperwork items do you currently have on the desk? 10? 20? 40 or more? For each item there is a message slip jumping up and down in your unconscious demanding attention. It is not hard to see how leaving unfinished paperwork on the desk can cause stress levels to shoot up.

As a reminder system the mental message slips perform rather haphazardly. They are constantly shooting into our conscious minds at inappropriate times. Equally, they remain in our unconscious during those times when we really need to be reminded of a particular message.

Consider the following scenario. A letter arrives from a client in the morning mail and you decide to reply to it that afternoon. The letter is placed on the desk where it soon disappears among the clutter, and you write out a mental message slip to yourself, "reply to clients letter today." The message slip is stored in your unconscious from whence it should surface at about 3:00 P.M. to remind you about the letter. However, you are extremely busy and your mind is occupied with other things. Driving home from work the message makes itself heard above the din and confused mass of your other reminders and you hear a scolding voice inside your head saying, "You forgot to reply to that letter, you will have to do it first thing tomorrow morning." On your journey into the office the next morning the message slip briefly pops into your conscious mind again screaming: "Remember to reply to the letter." A large pile of mail is waiting at the office and you are absorbed in dealing with it; then you go on to your morning meeting where the message slip surfaces to nag you once more. Later that night you are laying awake in bed and all of a sudden the thought flashes into your mind, "You forgot to reply to that letter again!"

This pattern of recurring reminders takes place every time we leave a piece of paper on our desks with the intention of dealing with it later.

What eventually happens to our mental message slips? Some of them are eliminated quite speedily if they are lucky enough to surface at the right time or if we spot the unfinished paperwork on the desk and deal with it. Other message slips, containing reminders to "start that project" can continue to nag us for weeks, months and even years, by which time they are hobbling around our unconscious with the aid of walking sticks, with barely enough energy to jump into our conscious mind. Eventually they fade away and die.

Mental message slips

The only way to stop mental message slips being produced is by writing down reminders in a place that the mind trusts. A loose piece of paper will not suffice because our unconscious knows that it will soon get lost on the desk. The answer lies in using a to-do list.

Why do so few people use a to-do list?
I doubt if there is an office worker anywhere in the world who has not at some time or other attempted to use a to-do list. Most of us would agree that the use of such lists is a good idea, in theory, but they don't seem to work in practice. Some of the most common problems I hear at my seminars are, "I never seem to be able to complete all the activities on my list"; "It is impossible to keep track of longer-term commitments";"I can't plan in my job, I have to be reactive and 'to-do' lists waste more time than they save."

Stated problem:"I never seem to be able to complete all the activities on my list."

*Actual problem:*You are attempting too much. In making your to-do lists you plan to fill up every moment of available time with activities. You leave no room for the interruptions and unexpected events that take up between 10 and 90 percent of any one day. Picture yourself in the office at 9:00 A.M. the morning after attending a time management seminar or reading a book on the subject. You have already produced a long to-do list in an attempt to clear practically the whole backlog of paperwork in one day. By 9:10 A.M. you have already drafted a reply to a letter you've been meaning to send for the past week. Fifteen minutes later you have quickly reviewed a report and produced a list of instructions for a colleague based on the report, which is now lying in your out-tray. By 9:40 A.M. you have dealt with a fax which had been clamoring for your attention for several days. Things are going well, you feel in control. Then the morning mail arrives. You deal with several items immediately, well, almost immediately, because you also have to take two phone calls. Then you are off to a meeting and on your return an urgent fax is awaiting your attention. After lunch a colleague drops in unexpectedly and you spend over an hour talking. It sounds like a pretty normal day for most of you, so far. Six P.M. comes and you look at your to-do list. Only five items have been checked off and there is still a huge backlog of important paperwork on your desk. Your enthusiasm for to-do lists disappears as you call home to apologize and say that you will be working late again. The next day you go back to your old routine of storing reminders on mental message slips. You know from experience the problems they cause but there does not seem to be an alternative that works.

Solution: Recognize and account for the fact that a large part of your day will be taken up with events you could not have foreseen. Many people plan the next day before they leave the office, but unexpected overnight faxes and some items in the morning mail will almost certainly require action that day. The best time to plan your day, therefore, is immediately after you have reviewed the mail. You will have a better idea of what you should be doing for the next eight hours.

Stated problem: "I can't plan in my job, I have to be reactive."

Actual problem: You are allowing others to dictate what paperwork you spend your time on. It seems that every time a colleague walks through the door with a piece of paper you end up dealing with it. While some of these interruptions are necessary, many are a waste of time. By adopting a "reactive" style you encourage others to bring their problems to you. The more urgent the problem or the larger the fire that has to be extinguished the better. However, while you are fighting fires, the stack of unfinished paperwork on your desk is leading to more fires. You never seem to have the time to prevent these fires from occurring. The more reactive you become the longer the line of people outside your door waiting for you to deal with their problems.

"I don't have time to plan—my job is very reactive"

Solution: It is time to sit down and take a close look at the paperwork that is landing on your desk. As you do, close your office door and divert your telephone calls temporarily. First of all make a list of all the important paperwork on your desk that requires action. Everything else should be filed away, given back to the people who dumped it on your desk in the first place or thrown into the trash. Over the next couple of days set aside some time to engage in a personal planning session. Decide where you want to be in five years time, in one year, in one month. Decide what you need to get there. You might find that achieving your long-term goals will leave you little time to take on the unnecessary paperwork of others. In the future beware of unnecessary interruptions. Use the important/urgent model introduced in Chapter 4 to evaluate incoming paperwork. Set aside one hour in the day, a "No interruptions" hour, that will immediately send the message to others that you are no longer willing to jump as soon as they shout "urgent." You will probably find them well able to cope with their own problems without you. You can now begin to start using a to-do list. Even if the nature of your job involves a high number of interruptions, you will find a to-do list useful as a reminder of the commitments you have made to others during those interruptions.

Stated Problem: "To-do lists waste more time than they save."

Actual problem: You waste so much time looking for your to-do list among the clutter on the desk, when you want to add to or refer to the list, that it is not possible to use it effectively. In the course of a normal day you might want to locate the list 15 to 20 times. Your problems have not ended even when you do manage to find the to-do list because then you have to search for the paperwork that the list has reminded you to tackle. A cluttered desk and a to-do list are not a good mix.

Solution: It is the clutter on our desks which is the cause of the wasted time, not the to-do list. If you make a note of your paperwork commitments as they occur, compiling a to-do list should not take up more than a few minutes a day. Many people are averse to using lists in the first place, but they will often write reminders to themselves on loose bits of paper which soon get lost. Apart from your current project, the to-do list, in a personal organizer, should be the only item on your desk. You will find a to-do list far easier to use if you are working from a clear desk.

Stated problem: "I can never keep track of future activities."

Actual problem: You may use just one to-do list for the day's paperwork and as a result you have no effective way of reminding yourself of an activity that has to be completed in the future. If you write it down on your current list, it will have been discarded long before the date when you need reminding. If you leave the paperwork on the desk to remind you, it will soon get buried. If you rely on memory you will experience the mental message slip problems discussed previously and it will almost certainly be forgotten.

Solution: The best way to overcome this problem is to use a to-do list for each day of the current week, along with a master list for each week and each month. If a letter arrives on your desk on Monday, the 7th and requires a reply on Thursday, the 10th, go to your to-do list for the 10th and write a reminder to yourself to complete the activity. If the letter requires a reply next week, go to your master list for next week and write it down. At the beginning of each week you should check your week's master list and transfer reminders to specific days. If the letter requires a reply next month, write a reminder on your month master list. A quick glance at this list at the beginning of each week will allow you to transfer any reminders to the appropriate day.

Step 2: Decide what the pay-off will be from dealing with each item of paperwork on the to-do list.

Once you have learned to trap all paperwork reminders on a to-do list, you are ready to move on to the next stage: prioritizing the activities on that list.

The Pareto principle

The Pareto principle was first highlighted by an Italian economist, Vilfredo Pareto. The principle states that 80 percent of your results come from 20 percent of your activities. We can look at it another way, 80 percent of our results come from 20 percent of our paperwork. So if we have a 40-hour backlog of paperwork on the desk we can expect that eight hours of that backlog will lead to 80 percent of our results. The pay-off from the remaining 32 hours of the backlog, correspondingly, will be relatively low. Common sense tells us then that 80 percent of the paperwork that lands on the desk should be ignored, leaving us to concentrate on getting the important 20 percent right.

One of the major automobile manufacturers in the U.S. actually got its staff to put this principle into practice. An experimental group were asked to list all of the activities in which they were engaged during the day. They then chose the 20 percent of activities that led to the highest pay-off. For one month the staff spent all their time on those high pay-off tasks, ignoring everything else. It is not surprising that productivity improved dramatically.

The high pay-off paperwork of a chief executive

All of the executives I talked to have a very clear definition of where their priorities lie. Gerald Ratner, without hesitation says, "Just going through the shop figures and checking the ones which have unsatisfactory performance and looking at the trends in different towns, I can see why a shop is doing badly or why it is doing well and try and learn something from that." Sir Allen Sheppard is more succinct, which suggests a highly focused mind, "anything to do with profit or cash or anything that adds value to the business." Richard Branson's concern for the customer shows up in what he considers to be high pay-off paperwork. He will read every letter that is addressed to him, a load which averages some 700 a week. He also places a high priority on reading the visitors book from the first class seating area of Virgin Airways, which contains comments from every passenger.

DEFINING YOUR OWN PRIORITIES

At a cluttered desk much of our time is spent doing the wrong things. If you are among that group of people who pay great attention to detail you are worse off because you are wasting even more time doing the wrong things well! You attentively read reports which should have never arrived on your desk in the first place. You draft and redraft memos which contain messages that should have been communicated verbally. The maximum pay-off comes from doing the right things well.

To identify the right things you need to assign priorities to every piece of paper that lands on your desk. The notation that people find to be most practical is the ABC notation. High pay-off paperwork is assigned an A priority, medium pay-off paperwork a B priority and low pay-off items a C priority. The exercise below is designed to help you to identify your own A, B and C priorities.

DEFINING YOUR PRIORITIES

What are your A priorities?
If you follow the Pareto principle, no more than 20 percent of the paperwork that lands on your desk should be assigned an A priority. There are three criteria you can use to help you to identify your A priorities.

1. Profit paperwork: "Anything to do with profit or cash."
What paperwork that you tackle has a major impact on the profit of your organization? It may be client enquiry forms which will lead to an increase in revenue or a market research report on the proposed launch of a new product. It might be a letter of complaint from a client, which if acted upon would lead to changes that would mean more people buying your product. But revenue enhancement is only one side of the coin; cost avoidance will also lead to greater profit. Included in this category might be a contract with a supplier or the examination of standard forms with the objective of eliminating them. The profit paperwork that you deal with will of course depend on the job you do. However, many companies and individuals are unaware of what paperwork really has an effect on profit. They often think they know, but upon closer examination, realize that the customer complaints they had been ignoring can or have lead to their downfall.

List the profit paperwork that passes across your desk under each of these headings:

(a) Revenue enhancement paperwork
(b) Cost avoidance paperwork

2. Deadline paperwork.

If you have made a commitment to deal with paperwork by a certain time or date, getting the paperwork done must always be an A priority. Deadline paperwork may include a special report that you have agreed to complete by a certain date or information you have promised a client. If you miss a deadline you can only use the classic excuse "I've been so busy" once without negative effects. As it becomes a habit your professional reputation suffers, your colleagues will bypass you if there is anything important to be done and your clients will deal with one of your competitors who is less busy. Self-imposed deadlines can become powerful motivators but if you constantly let them slip by, there is no point in setting them. Unrealistic deadlines should never be assigned an A priority. We have all worked with people who are constantly rushing around with urgent paperwork and need to have everything done yesterday. In fact the deadline may be weeks away or the urgency of the paperwork is a direct result of it lying on their desk for too long. Here again a notice in your office stating, "The lack of planning on your part does not constitute a crisis on my part," will get the message across to these people. Finally, deadline paperwork can include routine paperwork. It might be processing a stack of forms or completing a monthly report; if it is necessary to have this type of paperwork, it is necessary to complete it on time.

What deadline paperwork do you currently have on the desk?

(a) Self-imposed deadline paperwork
(b) Paperwork deadlines agreed with others
(c) Routine paperwork deadlines

3. Long-term projects or goals.

In the cut and thrust of daily office life the temptation is always to forego paperwork that will help you to achieve long-term goals and objectives and concentrate on more immediate, lower pay-off items. The story below, told to me by one chief executive I interviewed, illustrates the point well.

The elephant and the files

There were two shipwrecked sailors on a raft in the middle of the ocean. Their ship had gone down two weeks previously and they had not eaten for five days. Suddenly, one of the sailors spotted an island on the horizon and they paddled furiously to reach it. The first thing they thought about upon reaching dry land was food. Unfortunately there appeared to be only two forms of life on the island, thousands of flies that were buzzing around their heads and the tracks of a solitary elephant in the sand. The first sailor immediately grabbed a plank from the raft and began chasing flies. At first he was successful with a high headcount of about 50 flies an hour, but what he didn't realize was that the energy he was using up in catching each fly was greater than the calorie intake from the subsequent meal. As a result he soon wasted away. What of the second sailor? His first action was to sit down on the beach and plan how he would capture the elephant. His plan complete, he fashioned spears from the mast of the raft and carefully built a trap for the elephant. He was growing more hungry by the minute but he resisted the temptation to chase the flies that were constantly flying above his head. He knew he was weak and his only chance of success was to attack the elephant when it was at its most vulnerable. As the creature was sleeping, he attacked from behind and was successful. He

The fly swatter

was well fed for the next five weeks, after which time he was rescued by a passing ship.

In the office, elephant hunting and fly swatting are the two types of behavior we can exhibit when dealing with paperwork. The fly swatter is always extremely busy with lots of paperwork on the desk. Memos, faxes and message slips are constantly arriving on the desk, all warning of impending crises. The fly swatter is able to process up to a hundred pieces of paper a day but he can often be heard saying, as he takes another stress pill from the bottle on his desk, "I am always so busy but I don't seem to be accomplishing anything." The elephant hunter, on the other hand, has a focused mind and a clear desk. He hunts high pay-off paperwork and discards the rest of the incoming paperwork. He will often deal with only four or five pieces of paper in the day but he always leaves the office knowing that he has achieved something. As he drives past the office late at night he will see the fly swatter still at his desk struggling to get to grips with his backlog of paperwork.

It is important to break down longer-term goals or projects into step-by-step action plans. Any paperwork that will help us to achieve long-term goals should immediately be identified and assigned an A priority.

List your elephant-hunting paperwork.

What are your C priorities?

The bulk of the paperwork that lands on your desk should either be passed on or consigned to the trash straight away. This category includes all junk mail. Make sure you have a very broad definition of the work "junk." Ninety percent of the memos you receive will also belong in this category. In Chapter 3 you will have identified all the unnecessary paperwork that arrives on your desk. Most of that paperwork will not result in a pay-off high enough to justify dealing with it for any longer than the time it takes to dump it.

Make a list of the the C priority paperwork that commonly gets your attention because you have failed to discard it straight away.

Step 3: When deciding what paperwork to tackle next you should choose the item on your to-do list that will give you the highest pay-off.

If you produce a prioritized to-do list every day you are well on the way to maximizing your pay-off from the time you spend on paperwork. However, one final hurdle has to be overcome. That is the elimination of habits you have acquired over the years to help you decide what piece of paper to tackle next. The four main habits are discussed below. Every time you catch yourself slipping back into one of these unproductive behavior patterns, stop and pick up your to-do list.

Top-down approach

Here, the what to tackle next decision is influenced by whatever is at the top of the nearest pile of paper on your desk. You work from the top down and as soon as you spot something that requires your attention you pick it up and deal with it. This approach might work if the stack was sorted in order of decreasing pay-off, but invariably your most important paperwork is stuck at the bottom of the stack. By the time you get there it is too late to do anything about it and another opportunity has been missed. "But I always keep my important paper-work at the top of the stack," we tell ourselves. Not so.

Picture the process of sorting through the morning mail. The first letter you open is one which requires a speedy response; you therefore place it on the top of the stack in your in-tray to remind you to deal with it. But then as you go through the rest of the mail several other letters land on top of the stack, including many which you are not sure what to do with and are left on the desk as a way of delaying the decision. Throughout the day reports, memos, magazine articles and other items of paperwork arrive and by 5 P.M. your important letter is two-thirds of the way down the stack, practically eliminating its chances of being acted upon, for several days. If someone reminded you about the letter you would no doubt remember that it was in the stack, but you could just as easily forget. Your to-do list should replace the piles of paper on the desk as a reminder of what needs to be done. The top-down approach should be used only to work through your list, from your highest priority to your lowest priority.

Top-down approach

Distractions

The cluttered desk is made up of a lot of individual pieces of paper all clamoring for your attention. What item is tackled next is often based upon suddenly spotting a piece of paper that needs attention, often while you are in the middle of something else. You seem to be constantly switching from one item to another, leaving a trail of unfinished items on the desktop as you become engrossed in the distraction. That unfinished paperwork will then continually distract you, reminding you that it needs to be completed. Any loose piece of paper on your desk that requires action should be placed in one of your action files, with a corresponding note on your to-do list.

Pressure from others

The decision about what to tackle next is often made for you by others charging towards your desk with paperwork for your attention. More often than not, the interrupting paperwork has a lower pay-off than items already on the desk. Having a prioritized to-do list in front of you will give you greater control over interruptions. You can decide immediately, by referring to your list whether or not you have the time to deal with the interruption.

Procrastination

The desire to avoid uncomfortable paperwork often plays a major role in deciding what you will do next. You can often waste a whole day dealing with low pay-off but interesting paperwork while important paperwork remains undone. If the desk is clear, you don't have the stack of low pay-off, but interesting paperwork on hand, that will ease your feelings of guilt as you procrastinate. You have to make a conscious decision to locate unimportant paperwork with which to waste your time. Every morning you should be aware of all your A priority paperwork for the day and you should tackle nothing else until those items have been completed.

CHAPTER SIX

Clear Your Filing System!

If you are delegating properly you should be able to live within a certain number of filing cabinets. If you begin to see those filing cabinets grow, then unless there has been a fantastic change in the nature of the organization, it's a sign that something is getting out of control. I have an annual purge to restructure the system and I say, "What's essential? What shall we keep? Who else holds papers on this topic? Do we really need this?" I'm fairly ruthless about chucking stuff out.

— Professor George Bain

SIR ALLEN SHEPPARD, chief executive of Grand Metropolitan, should have every right to be suffocating under mountains of files and records. He runs a seventeen billion dollar company with over 140,000 people reporting to him, but as he describes, everything is under control:

> *We don't keep files in the office apart from a blue file of everything we issue and action files on each director. These current action files are reviewed every time there is a meeting. I draw up an agenda from current action points and everything that is killed as a result of that will be purged immediately and thrown away, so that at any moment the file should be relatively thin.*

Such ruthlessness is the key to faultless filing.

1893 is one of those dates which is recorded in the annals of paperwork management. At the Chicago World Fair in that year, the vertical filing system was introduced for the first time. Loose pieces of paper could be filed in tabbed folders along with other documents relating to the same subject. Items could be exchanged between one folder and another almost at will, and new subject categories could be introduced simply by adding another tabbed folder. It was a huge advantage over the traditional methods of filing. However, as we approach the hundreth anniversary of this great innovation, we are still struggling to come to grips with it.

Two of the problems that we encounter today surfaced almost immediately. Whereas prior to 1893 very little internal correspondence survived beyond its initial use. The introduction of the new filing system meant that instead of being discarded, unnecessary paperwork could now be kept for years. The second problem that led to the proliferation of stored paper was the question of documents which related to more than one subject. The solution was to duplicate the information so that a copy could be filed in each category. An internal memo from the Dupont company, dating back to 1901, illustrates the problem and the unfortunate solution:

> *In order that the new system of filing our correspondence (vertical files) which I have adopted in my office here, may be effective, it is essential that each subject corresponded about should be included in a separate letter, as when two or more subjects are written about in the same letter, it is necessary for extracts to be made of each for the different files.*

This memo should of course have been discarded upon receipt but it has survived for nearly 90 years.

The statistics on filing are alarming:

- We spend 9.2 percent of our time searching for information on the desk or in the filing system, which is approximately 45 minutes a day or 19 days a year.
- People ignore up to 85 percent of the documents they retain.
- 45 percent of the documents we file are already filed elsewhere.

- Canadian business spends $500 million per annum to store over 170 million cubic meters of paper.
- In the U.S. there are over 300 billion documents on file with another 76 billion being added every year.
- Each white collar worker in Europe hoards over 20,000 pieces of paper; they generate 5,000 new pieces of paper every year but discard only 3,000.
- A U.S. study estimated that it costs $25,000 to print and process the forms in each four-drawer filing cabinet, $2,160 annually to maintain each cabinet.

HOW EFFECTIVE IS YOUR FILING SYSTEM?

The 20 questions below will help you to identify your filing strengths and weaknesses. Place a check in the box for each statement you agree with.

1. I often allow "to-file" paperwork to build up on the desk and I only get around to dealing with it when there is no more room left on the desk. ☐

2. I often have difficulty deciding what subject category to file under. ☐

3. I tend to leave paperwork on the desk rather than file it away, when I intend to work on it the same day. ☐

4. If I was absent from the office my colleagues would have great difficulty trying to locate information in my filing cabinets. ☐

5. My filing system has grown in response to day-to-day requirements, I never

consciously planned a classification system to suit my needs.   ☐

6. My filing system contains documents which I rarely refer to and that could quite easily be located elsewhere.   ☐

7. My filing system contains obsolete files.   ☐

8. I have not cleared out my filing system in the past six months.   ☐

9. I often file away material for future reference but never use it again.   ☐

10. On average, I spend more than 20 minutes a day trying to locate documents from my desktop and filing system.   ☐

11. I sometimes have to complete a report from memory because I have lost a draft or notes.   ☐

12. I have been known to file current action paperwork away and then forget about it.   ☐

13. I often go into meetings unprepared because I have not been able to locate the background paperwork.   ☐

14. I have huge stacks of reading material building up around me in the office.   ☐

15. When a project has been successfully completed I do not purge the project file.   ☐

16. The labels in my filing system frequently cause confusion. ☐

17. There are a large number of folders in
my filing cabinet that are bulging
with excess paperwork. ☐

18. I have knowingly filed documents in
the wrong folder because it was too
much trouble to find the correct one. ☐

19. I have one drawer in my filing cabinet
which is used as a dump drawer. ☐

20. I frequently lose pieces of paper that
should have been filed. ☐

THE HOARDING HABIT

We just don't like to throw things away. We are afraid
that as soon as we discard a document someone will
charge into the office demanding to see it. One of the
major rationalizations we use in hoarding piles of
unnecessary paper is, "I don't have time to work on it
now, but I will, in a few months' time." Invariably we
never do get around to dealing with it. Vast quantities
of paperwork find its way into our filing systems for
reference purposes, but we never refer to it. We also store
irrelevant memos and reports which are never read or
are obsolete anyway. The "keep a copy" syndrome is
entrenched in the culture of almost every organization.
The rumor that many government departments
photocopy all documents before they are discarded is
probably not far from the truth and could well apply
throughout industry.

The cost of keeping unnecessary information is
enormous, but few companies focus on this as an area

for cost savings. In Canada, it has been estimated that companies store over 170 million cubic meters of paper at a cost of $500 million. What are the costs of being ruthless with paper? What is the worst thing that could happen if a document was discarded that was subsequently required? Those who are committed discarders report that this rarely happens. But if it did, what would happen? If the document was an internal one, there is probably a 90 percent chance that a copy of the document could be located within 200 feet of the first. If the document originated from outside the organization there may be only a two-day delay to have a copy sent by mail.

Most company filing manuals positively encourage individuals to keep information rather than throw it away. They list "where" and "how" to file every document imaginable rather than advising individuals to keep only what they need. The Marks & Spencer's principle "when in doubt, throw it out" is a good one to adopt. After their "Operation Simplification" over 1,000 filing cabinets were sold off because they were no longer necessary. A common sense rule of filing is that "files expand to fill the space available." Why not experiment with the introduction of smaller filing cabinets in your company or, better still, eliminate filing cabinets altogether in certain departments.

FILING DISORDER

Our filing systems tend to expand in response to day-to-day needs, without any careful thought or planning. Retrieving paperwork from the filing system is often akin to the launch of a major expedition. First of all there is a frustrating search to locate the correct folder. We are confused by our own file labels and we can't remember what label we filed under. The folder may not be in the filing cabinet but somewhere around the office or on the desk of one of our colleagues. When we do manage to locate the correct folder it is often bulging with unnecessary paperwork and we have to undertake a further search to extract the correct document.

Because of disorganization in our filing cabinets, paperwork which should have been filed builds up on our desk or underneath it. The mental effort required to decide where to file a document in a poorly classified system means that we delay filing until there is no more room on or around the desk to store documents. The fear that filing documents away will mean losing them is also a very powerful motivator to hoard "to-file" paperwork on the desktop. It only takes a second to place a piece of paper on top of a stack on the desk but it can take us hours actually to find it again a few days later! In fact, over an average working lifetime we spend in the region of 800 working days trying to locate information on our desk or in the filing system.

THE TWO APPROACHES TO FILING

However much unnecessary paperwork we hoard in our filing systems, they do contain valuable information: important ideas and plans which will contribute towards our future success, opportunities for new business, information vital to the maintenance of good relation ships with clients and suppliers, and records which will safeguard us against future threats. A filing system is effective if it allows us to retrieve that important information, quickly and easily.

Filing traditionally has been seen as a physical, clerical activity, the chief purpose of which is the storage of information. As a result there has been little concern over the amount of information retained—"If we have the space then don't throw it away." The stacks of to-file paperwork have built up on our desk because the act of filing is seen as a demeaning activity, with little real pay-off.

The second and more effective approach sees filing as a conceptual, managerial activity, the chief purpose of which is the quick and easy retrieval of information. Information is seen as a valuable strategic resource and the harder it is to locate, the less valuable it becomes. Great care should be taken in the design of a filing system in order to minimize the time spent retrieving information.

Priority filing
Each piece of paper on or around the desk has a particular activity rating that is determined by the frequency with which we pick it up and when we next need to work on it. We will refer to our to-do list 15 or 20 times a day to add reminders or to decide what to do next. It therefore has a high activity rating. A fax which arrives on the desk that requires a response the same day will have a lower activity rating, and a supplier's catalog we use once a month will be lower still. If we are to reduce the overall time we spend searching for paperwork it is sensible to make the items with a higher activity rating more accessible.

The priority filing model below has three levels. Level 1 includes all the high activity paperwork, to-do lists, calendars, project overviews and communication files on key people. These items should all be filed on the desktop in a personal organizer. Level 2 includes all the medium activity paperwork, which includes all our "act-on" paperwork, divided into four categories: correspondence, meetings, reading and projects. These documents are held in our current action files. Level 3 includes all the documents that we have already tackled or that we need to keep for reference purposes. These are stored in our filing cabinet.

Level 1: Desktop filing

At any one time, your personal organizer and the paperwork you are currently dealing with should be the only two items on your desktop. Your personal organizer should be used as a fast access filing system for key information on your commitments, activities, to-do items, communications, ideas, plans, projects and meetings. There are many good organizers on the market, not all of them expensive. The important thing is to develop a system that suits your needs and stick to it, religiously.

Keeping track of your commitments is relatively straightforward. The personal organizer you choose should allow you to produce a to-do list every day plus master to-do lists for each week and month. A detachable calendar is also a necessity so that your personal organizer does not have to travel with you on social engagements. All message slips and Post-it™ notes should be trapped by your personal organizer. If you have been away from your desk and several message slips have been left for your attention, transfer the details to your daily to-do list on your return and discard the loose bits of paper. This is slightly less efficient than keeping the message slips but far more effective because it means that loose pieces of paper will not be lying around the desk to distract you. It also means they won't get lost.

Each of your long-term projects and goals should be summarized on one page to give you an overview against which you can check your progress. Each project should be broken down into individual steps which can then be scheduled on your daily to-do lists. Similarly, each meeting you attend should be assigned a separate page on which you can note down ideas as you prepare and keep track of decisions made during the meeting.

A record of your communication with the key people around you both within the organization and externally is essential. For those of you who spend most of your time at your desks, incorporating a "talk to" system in your personal organizers can be useful. Each of your clients or contacts should have one page on which everything you need to say, have said or that has been said to you, should be noted down. If you receive a call from an important client it is useful to be able to turn to that client's page and review who said what the last time you spoke to someone in that organization and be reminded of something important you need to discuss with them. We have all experienced those telephone calls when we knew there was something important we wanted to say to the other person but we couldn't remember exactly what it was. Then the instant we put down the telephone receiver we remember and a repeat phone call is necessary. If you make a series of commitments to someone during a telephone call or a meeting, and you do not write them down, within half an hour you will have forgotten at least one of the things you said you would do. It is important to write things down.

Level 2: Current action files
Paperwork that we need to tackle in the near future is normally dealt with in one or two ways, either it is left on the desktop where it is soon hidden and forgotten, or placed in the filing cabinet where it is forgotten. A third alternative, which is the only way to deal with current action paperwork, is to temporarily store it in holding files. You should set up action files with the following headings: "meetings," "correspondence," "projects" and "reading." It may be appropriate to set up

separate current action files for large projects or key individuals and you may find it useful to use a bring forward file to hold items that are activated by date. Start by using the four main current action files and then experiment to find a system that suits you. Because you will be adding to and extracting from the action files several times a day it is important to keep them in an accessible place. A desk-side drawer is most suitable but if you don't have one, place them at the front of the easiest drawer to reach in your filing cabinet.

Correspondence current action file
The purpose of this file is to temporarily store your incoming and outgoing correspondence. This can include letters, memos and faxes. We normally deal with incoming mail by glancing at it and placing it in the in-tray. When it gets acted upon is often determined by when it eventually reaches the top of the stack. If you looked through your in-tray at this moment there would almost certainly be several letters which should have been dealt with long before now.

Each morning as you are sorting through the mail, place the correspondence file on the desk. One by one the letters should be assigned a priority, A for high pay-off, B for medium pay-off and C for low pay-off. The act on, pass on, file or discard process is then applied. If you choose to act, then decide on a time or date and write a reminder of this on the appropriate to-do list. Place the letter in your correspondence file and move on to the next letter. This file can also be used for holding drafts of outgoing letters while they await approval or further thought. The faxes that litter our desks can also be stored here until we act on them. Most incoming memos should be discarded as soon as you read them, but on the occasion of further action being required they should be placed in your correspondence file.

Meeting current action file

How often do you attend meetings at which the objectives have not been achieved because of paperwork problems? The agenda has not been distributed in time, some preparatory paperwork has not been completed or you cannot find the background paperwork and you sit through the meeting completely lost. The vast majority of time spent at meetings is completely wasted because of problems with paperwork. Meetings are frequently seen as a chance to become acquainted with the subject rather than doing any preparation work by reading the background material. Meetings should end in decisions being made but so often the parting shot is "let's go away and think about it." Any thinking should have been done before the meeting.

Depending on your schedule the background paperwork should be gathered together one or two days prior to the meeting. Set aside time to review the paperwork and write down any ideas or thoughts you have about the meeting. Place the paperwork in your meeting current action file and this will prevent any last minute frantic searches to locate it. A useful rule of thumb is to spend less time at unnecessary meetings and more time preparing paperwork for the important ones.

Project current action file

Projects can involve anywhere from one to several hundred items of paperwork. The danger with larger projects is that the paperwork often slips through the cracks because you have been busy "fly swatting" with immediate pay-off paperwork. Each time project-related paperwork lands on the desk you need to be aware of when it needs to be completed by in order for the project to proceed smoothly. Set a deadline to deal with paperwork before it is needed and write it down on the appropriate to-do list. Place the paperwork in your project current action file until it is required. For larger projects you may have a master folder in your filing cabinet. This should only be used for completed or reference paperwork. Some people find it useful to use several project action folders or one folder with several subdivisions. If you are dealing with a large amount of paperwork relating to only a few projects, this system will be beneficial to you.

Reading current action file
Reports, magazines, brochures, newsletters and catalogs provide a never ending stream of reading material. However, there is only a certain amount of information that we can take in. At an average reading speed for light material of 250 words a minute, we could only get through 300 pages a day. Our reading therefore needs to be carefully prioritized. You may find it better to use a box file for capturing reading material; a simple wallet file will only take a few magazines or reports.

Set aside specific reading periods two or three times a week. If a magazine lands on your desk, place it in your reading file. You should resist the temptation to pick up a magazine and read it through from cover to cover. Scan the contents and check off articles which are of interest. If you have time after reading the high-priority articles you may choose to explore further. Alternatively, you may scan through magazines as they reach you and tear out or photocopy articles to be placed in your reading file. Then throw the magazine away. By keeping all your reading material in one place you do not have to search among stacks on the desk to find items to read while traveling. When your reading file becomes full it is time to purge it. Discard the low pay-off material and prune the file back to about 50 percent full.

Level 3: Clear you filing cabinet!

CLEAR YOUR
FILING CABINET! ACTION PLAN

This action plan can be carried out individually but is more often completed by groups of people within a department or the company as a whole as part of a special Clear Your Desk! Day. The objectives are threefold:

- To clear out all unnecessary paperwork from your filing system by discarding it, passing it on or by acting on it.
- To reorganize your files so that the time you spend trying to locate documents in your filing system will be reduced.
- To enable you to identify your filing bad habits and to take steps to ensure that they are eliminated.

Block out as much time in your diary as you think is necessary to try and ensure that you are not interrupted during the clearout. You should set aside at least one hour for each drawer in your filing cabinet. Half-way through the process you will be looking actively for alternative activities to use as an excuse to put it off until tomorrow but try and stick with it; your perseverance will be well rewarded. Ensure that you have replacement stationery elements, such as hanging files, wallets, file tabs and so on, on hand before you start. Bags, waste baskets or recycling boxes should be handed out to all the participants in the clearout.

1. Set a target
If it is more than six months since you last had a major

clearout of your filing system, then you should aim to discard about 70 percent of the paperwork in your cabinet. Remember that 85 percent of the documents we retain are ignored anyway, so even if you throw out three-quarters of the documents there will still be many left that you will never use again. Be absolutely ruthless. If in doubt, throw it out. Use Sir Allen Sheppard's filing system as an ideal to aim for. Don't set your standards against the overflowing filing systems of your colleagues. One manager I know starts clearouts with the intention of throwing everything away. Only as he goes through his files does he relent and pick out documents which he really needs to retain. Shout down the little voice inside your head that is telling you not to throw anything out "because you may need it someday."

If you are organizing a company clearout, set a target for the company as a whole. We store an average of 20,000 pieces of paper in our filing systems. If there are 100 people taking part and each throws away 70 percent of their stored documents, the total figure will reach 14 million pieces of paper!

2. Set up current action files
Set aside three folders and label them "correspondence," "meetings" and "projects." Obtain a box file and label it "reading." Decide where you are going to keep these files. A desk-side drawer is the most appropriate for the first three action files and your reading file should be placed on top of the filing cabinet.

3. Open each drawer of your filing cabinet and ask yourself the following questions:

- Is my filing system overflowing with unnecessary paper?

- Are there subject folders bulging with excess documents, that could easily be subdivided into smaller categories?
- Have I retained files which are clearly obsolete?
- Are there folders containing almost no paper that could be merged under a broader subject category?
- Can I tell immediately by looking at each file label what the file contains?
- Are there several files with the same or similar subject labels that cause confusion?
- Is there an obvious classification system or are my files organized in a haphazard fashion?
- Are my files organized in a way that allows quick and easy retrieval of information?
- Are the stationery items in my filing system in need of replacement: hanging files, file tabs, wallets?
- Is my filing system poorly organized because I lack the correct stationery elements?
- Are there stacks of paper in some of my file drawers that have just been dumped there?

Rate yourself on the following scales:

Discarder .... Hoarder

Hopelessly disorganized .... Well organized

Stationery dates back to 1893 .... Stationery in good order

4. Remove obsolete files
If there are files which contain obsolete information, discard them en masse. This step alone will eliminate a large proportion of your stored paper. Obsolete files include failed projects, projects which never got off the ground, records of employees who have left the company, suppliers you no longer do

business with and clients who no longer do business with you. You may come across files which would be more appropriately stored elsewhere perhaps because someone has taken over an area of responsibility.

5. Purge the remaining folders

Take each folder out of the filing cabinet and place it on the desk. Does the folder contain valuable information? How frequently do you refer to each folder? Why? The act-on, pass-on, file or discard decision process is also useful for deciding the fate of your filed documents. Work through the stack of documents in each folder and make five stacks on the desk: (a) act-on; (b) pass-on; (c) discard: (d) refile in current folder; (e) refile in another folder. Any documents that are refiled should be marked with a discard date. Any documents that have been misfiled should be left on on the desk until later (step 10 of the action plan). If you file them straight away you will probably come across them again as you clear out your other folders.

6. Act-on paperwork

There is always a great temptation to deal with "act-on" items as you come across them. Try to resist it. If you start making telephone calls or writing letters while you still have several stacks to sort out on the desk, I guarantee you will lose what you are working on. When you have gone through every folder you will be aware of exactly what needs to be done and you will be in a better position to set priorities. Work through the act-on stack from the top down assigning priorities to each item. Create two further stacks: A priority and B priority. Take each "A" item and decide when you are going to tackle it and make a note of this on the relevant to-do list. Then work through the "B" stack and do the same.

7. Pass-on paperwork

"Pass-on" paperwork includes both paperwork that belongs in the filing system of someone else and paperwork that requires action and you have decided to delegate it. If you think the documents are more appropriately filed elsewhere, before you do anything ask the person who will receive the files if they want or need them. Mark any delegated item clearly with instructions for the delegatee. If you are completing the clearout as part of a group, identify documents that are frequently duplicated by each person in the group but which could easily be located in central files.

8. Discard paperwork

This should form the largest stack on your desk. If your target is to reduce the stored paper you will need to discard an average of seven documents out of every ten in each folder. The following guidelines may help you to decide what to discard:

- As you work through project folders, discard any background paperwork for projects that have been completed successfully.
- Copies of documents that have been placed in several files should be eliminated; keep the document in the most relevant file.
- Any documents you filed more than six months ago that you had intended to deal with "someday" should be discarded.
- Reference documents that are never referred to or are now out of date should also end up in the trash.
- For each document ask yourself, "what is the worst thing that could happen if I threw this

out?" If you can live with the consequences, then go ahead and throw it out.

9. Develop a suitable classification system

The key to rapid retrieval of information from your filing system is a good classification system. Most of us will have had a vague system in mind when we set up our filing system but it is likely to have grown in directions we couldn't have foreseen. The result is a mass of files with no apparent order. Take a blank piece of paper and make a list of all the files currently in your filing cabinet, and using the guidelines below design a classification that best suits your retrieval needs. There are six main ways of classifying files:

By subject category: It is straightforward logic to keep documents which contain similar types of information together in one file. In setting subject categories you should beware of defining the category too narrowly. Instead of setting up separate files for market research, advertising and PR you might start off with one file for marketing and then subdivide the category as the file gets bigger. So you might end up with Marketing: Advertising; Marketing: Research ...

Alphabetically: Subject categories are normally arranged alphabetically for ease of retrieval. For example, Administration, Budgets, Clients and so on. It may be appropriate to set up a miscellaneous file under each letter to store documents until the setting up of a separate file is warranted.

By date: If people refer to certain documents by date rather than by subject then for ease of retrieval they should be filed in this manner. Incoming faxes are often filed in this manner.

By color: Files can be color coded to identify them as belonging to a particular category. Important clients could be filed with red tabs or in blue folders so they can be located quickly.

Activity rating: Frequently used files could be stored at the front of the file drawer. Current action files are stored according to this principle.

Numerically: This classification is often used where security is a priority. Files are ordered numerically with the key being an index which is constantly updated. The advantage of this system is that file tabs do not have to be changed as subject categories alter. This system, however, can be dangerous in the hands of a disorganized filer. If the index is not kept up to date, it becomes almost impossible to locate anything.

Once you have arrived at a suitable classification system you will need to change the tabs on your files to fit in with the new system. File labels should be kept short and simple. An elaborate heading which may seem appropriate when you are setting up a file may cause confusion at a later date. At this stage you may also need to replace file wallets or introduce them for new categories. You should also type up a copy of your new index to give you a good mental map of your system.

10. Reorganize files

With your classification system in order you will now need physically to reorganize your files to fit in with it. The contents of several files may be merged or the documents from bulging files split into thinner folders. You will still have a stack of documents on the desk which you had previously misfiled. Now is the time to refile correctly. If you have any trouble deciding where to file these documents, you should re-evaluate your new classification system.

CHAPTER SEVEN

Clear Your Desk! - Action Plan

I went up to someone in my office who had a mountain of paperwork on the desk and [he] said, "I can't go on holiday because I have all this paperwork to clear. If I go on holiday, when I come back there will be even more!" I was unimpressed with that because I felt that if he couldn't organize a holiday with his wife and kids for two weeks then he was really not capable of running that department.

— Gerald Ratner

Clear Your Desk!
Action plan

THE OBJECTIVES OF this exercise are to help you to clear the unnecessary paper from your desktop and to win back control over your important paperwork. Rather than working through the action plan on your own you should encourage others in the office to join you. Better still organize an in-company Clear Your Desk! day and get everyone to stop work for two hours to clear the clutter from their desks.

Set aside two hours, undisturbed, to complete the process. It is important that you complete the Clear Your Filing System Action Plan before you start on the desk. Dealing with "to-file" paperwork on the desk will be far easier if you have an organized filing system. Before starting you should have your current action files—correspondence, reading, projects and meetings reading—ready to take the "act-on" paperwork from the desktop.

The clearout of the desk and filing system results in an average of 400 pieces of paper being eliminated. You will quite obviously need to arm yourself with several waste baskets and trash bags. If you are one of a large group undertaking this exercise you should set up a collection scheme to capture all recyclable paper. In 1987, the Body Shop launched "Project Paperchase" to ensure that all reclaimable office wastepaper was collected. The important features of their system are as follows:

1. Each desk (as far as is practical) has two trash bins, preferably of a different color; one is for reclaimable

paper, the other is for all other rubbish.

2. Each office zone has a project coordinator to check the consistent and proper segregation of reclaimable paper.

3. In each zone there is a central collecting bin into which every employee empties their own reclaimable paper.

4. Cleaning staff transfer the reclaimable paper to a single storage area to await collection by a contractor who transports it to a paper mill.

Recycling your discarded paperwork is both a socially and a financially rewarding exercise. However, it is far better not to photocopy unnecessary reports in the first place than to recycle the report once it has been discarded.

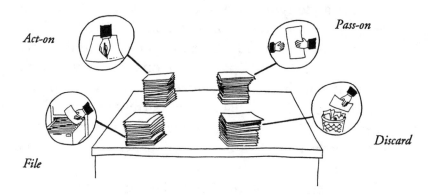

Act-on

Pass-on

File

Discard

CLEAR YOUR DESK! ACTION PLAN

1. Attacking the paperwork mountain

Sort through the mountain of paperwork on the desk and separate the "act-on, pass-on, file and discard" paperwork into four stacks (as shown in the illustration above). As you pick up each piece of paper from the desktop make a definite decision as to its fate, then place it in the correct stack. Try to complete this process without allowing yourself to be distracted. This is where most desk clearing efforts break down.

2. Work through the "act-on" stack

Work through the act-on stack from the top down. Decide when you will tackle each piece of paper and write a reminder to yourself on your to-do list for the relevant day. When you have done this, place the paperwork in the appropriate action file—correspondence, meetings, reading or projects. As you work through this stack you will undoubtedly come across paperwork that you are tempted to deal with immediately. Avoid telephoning the person whose name you discover on a Post-it™ note or drafting a reply to an important letter you come across, until the action plan has been completed. Those items would probably have remained hidden on the desktop anyway, had you not begun to sort out your paperwork. As you work through the stack remind yourself of Professor George Bain's advice:

> *I tend to have a rule that anything that comes in during the day goes out in the day. At least I get it off my desk and I take action on it. I think one of the main ways of creating work is to put aside small jobs. I find that if it's something you do right away then bang! that's it. Whereas if you say, I'll get around to it one of these days, it's just a minor matter, you create a whole pile of jobs for yourself.*

3. Work through the "pass-on" stack

There are three main categories of pass-on paperwork. The first is paperwork which should not have landed on your desk in the first place. It will include unnecessary reports, memos and all those "leave it with me" documents that you asked your colleagues to dump on your desk. Now is the time to return that paperwork to the person who left it on the desk. This should be done in a good natured way and you should explain to the person why you consider the items to be unnecessary. They may even be pleased to take your name off their circulation list for memos and reports. The objective of this exercise is to ease your paperwork burden, not to score political points over anyone. If you are taking part in an in-company Clear Your Desk! day don't be surprised if a large amount of paperwork that you have sent to others arrives back on your desk.

The second category of pass-on paperwork consists of the routine items such as your bosses' correspondence or standard forms of which you only process one part. This type of paperwork should never stay on your desk for a second longer than is necessary. The third category of pass-on paperwork includes all the paperwork you intend to delegate. Ensure that this paperwork does not land on someone else's desk without clear instructions. Agree on a completion deadline with the delegatee and make a note of it on the relevant date in your diary. There is no need to make a copy of the delegated paperwork; trust the delegatee not to lose it.

4. Work through the "file" stack
Once you have reorganized your filing system this step should not present any problems. Before you file each item ask yourself, "Do I really need to keep this?" Studies have shown that 85 percent of retained documents are never referred to and nearly 45 percent of retained documents are already filed somewhere else. You should never

file anything that will rarely be used and that can easily be located elsewhere. In the future ensure that the "to-file" stack does not build up on the desk. Items should be filed as soon as you have finished dealing with them or as soon as they arrive on the desk.

5. Deal with the "discard" stack

Pat yourself on the back as your pile of unwanted paper lands in the trash. Calculate the amount of time you have wasted in dealing with the items in the stack and make a pact with yourself to place these items directly in the trash in the future, rather than allowing them to build up on the desk. Think of the techniques discussed in this book that will help you to prevent this type of paperwork from reaching your desk from now on.

6. Eliminate multiple diaries

Many of us use a mish-mash of diary systems to help keep track of our to-do items, meetings, projects and communications. They include wall planners, desk diaries, pocket diaries, electronic diaries, computer diaries and an assortment of loose pieces of paper. The end result is often total confusion. Have you ever been in the situation where after a meeting a date is suggested for a follow up meeting and there is a sudden flurry of activity while diaries are pulled out of pockets, computer keyboards are being tapped, eyes are peering over your shoulder at wall planners, hands are rummaging through stacks to locate desk diaries ...After a few frantic minutes the person on the other side of the desk stops and says, "I'll have to get back to you to confirm it, I'm not sure of my schedule on that day."

The alternative to the above confusion is to keep everything in one place. Get a good personal organizer and use it religiously. Transfer all your fixed commitments and to-do items to your organizer straight away and discontinue your use of other systems.

7. Deal with stationery items

Collect all pens, pencils, rulers, paper clips and other stationery items and place them in a desktop holder or suitable drawer. If these items are scattered around the desk they add to the feeling of clutter. All blank pieces of paper including memo, notepads and Post-it™ notes should be thrown away. Your personal organizer should replace the functions they perform.

8. Remove your in-tray from the desk

If possible take your in-tray off the desk and place it behind you. Paperwork in the in-tray serves as a constant source of distraction and should be kept out of sight until you have time to decide on how to deal with it. The in-tray also serves as a convenient storage place for paperwork you are trying to put off.

9. Shelve reference books and manuals

Take all reference books, manuals and magazines off the desk and store them in an appropriate place. Magazines, if you really need to keep them should be stored in box files or special magazine files. Frequently used reference books should be kept in a desk-side drawer or other convenient place. Manuals should always be shelved when not in use.

10. Designate your office a clutter-free zone
Place a sign on your office door indicating that it is a clutter-free zone. Encourage others around you to do the same thing. The golden rule is to work on just one project at a time. One project may mean 20 pieces of paper are on the desk but as long as they are related to that project there will be no unnecessary distractions.

ORGANIZING AN IN-COMPANY CLEAR YOUR DESK! DAY

The Clear Your Desk! concept should not just be adopted by individuals who have bought this book or have attended a Clear Your Desk! seminar but by everyone in your organization. To that end you should designate one day every year to be Clear Your Desk! day. On that day everyone in the organization from chief executive down should stop work to undertake a clearout of their filing systems and desktop paperwork.

There is both a serious and a fun side to Clear Your Desk! day. The objectives of the day are to increase the awareness throughout the company of paperwork problems, to guide individuals towards winning back control over their paperwork and to act as a starting point in the war against bureaucratic paperwork. The actual clearout should be approached in a light-hearted way. Prizes could be awarded to departments or groups with the highest participation rate; before, during and after photographs could be taken for your company newsletter. One hundred office workers simultaneously clearing their desks in an open plan office is a sight to behold!

CLEAR YOUR DESK! DAY ACTION PLAN

1. Decide on the date for your in-company Clear Your Desk! day

International Clear Your Desk! Day takes place on the last Friday of April every year. Your in-company Clear Your Desk! day can be held on this day or another more suitable date. It is important that everyone participates, so avoid the day clashing with a busy sales period or when a large proportion of the office workers are on holiday. To ensure that the day is a success you will need to start planning at least three months in advance. Designating one day a year to managing paperwork ensures that attention is constantly focused on paperwork problems and that it will never become a "we looked at that a few years ago and sent some people on a course" issue. The attempt to control desktop paperwork and to ease the bureaucratic paperwork will become part of the culture of the organization.

2. Set up a Clear Your Desk! committee

The Clear Your Desk! committee should be set up several months in advance of Clear Your Desk! day. The committee should be made up of individuals from as many functions as is practical, the more senior the members the better. Reporting directly to the chief executive, the committee's main role is to ensure that the management of paperwork is assigned a high priority in the organization. Its members will be responsible for organizing and publicizing Clear Your Desk! day and also for reviewing corporate paperwork with a view to reducing the paperwork burden on the company's office workers.

3. Organize Clear Your Desk! seminars

The Clear Your Desk! organization runs in-house seminars on managing paperwork. These seminars are of two types. The day long Clear Your Desk! seminar should be attended by key managers in the organization, those who have a significant level of control over the paperwork that flows across the desk. The one hour motivational Clear Your Desk! seminar focuses on the techniques for managing personal paperwork and is often held to introduce individuals to the Clear Your Desk! concept. Departments or groups of people who work together should attend the seminar together so that the effective management of paperwork becomes a team effort. Companies wishing to arrange Clear Your Desk! seminars should contact the Clear Your Desk! Organization, 27 Old Gloucester Street, London WC1N 3XX, Tel: 081 903 7261.

4. Make contact with paper merchants

Those companies who have to date organized in-company Clear Your Desk! days have found that an average of 400 pieces of paper were discarded from each desktop. If your company has 1,000 office workers it would produce a stack of close to half a million pieces of reclaimable paper. Paper merchants should be contacted well in advance of Clear Your Desk! day to negotiate a price for the waste paper and to arrange for its efficient collection.

5. Appoint Clear Your Desk! coordinators

A coordinator should be appointed for each department branch office or group of office workers. The job of the coordinator is to spread information about the event within his or her own group, to motivate people to take part to ensure that everything goes smoothly on the day.

6. Publicize the Clear Your Desk! day
Write an article in your company newsletter telling people about the event, explaining why it is taking place and what people are expected to do. Posters announcing Clear Your Desk! day are available from the Clear Your Desk! Organization and these should be placed on notice boards and walls throughout the company. The event could be launched by organizing a Clear Your Desk! presentation at a company conference.

7. Distribute copies of this book to all those taking part
Ensure that every office worker receives a copy of this book at least two weeks before Clear Your Desk! day to give them an understanding of the reasons behind it.

8. Clear Your Desk! day
On Clear Your Desk! day, every office worker from the chief executive down should take part in the clearout. It may take some well organized individuals less than an hour to clear their desks and filing systems but nobody should act as if they are above the whole thing. Everyone who participates will benefit. Internal meetings and telephone calls should be kept to a minimum.

Between 10:00 A.M. and 1:00 P.M. individuals should work through the Clear Your Filing System Action Plan. The group coordinators should be on hand to collect waste paper and to provide stationery elements that are needed such as hanging files, tabs and wallets. Current action files labeled correspondence, meetings, readings and projects should be prepared and handed out to each individual.

Between 2:00 P.M. and 4:00 P.M. the Clear Your Desk! Action plan should be followed. Group coordinators should be familiar with both action plans so they can guide people through them.

9. Start the purge on bureaucratic paperwork

Clear Your Desk! day is not the end of the Clear Your Desk! process. The Clear Your Desk! committee should now focus its attention on reducing the level of bureaucratic paperwork in the organization. The action plans given in chapter 3 for eliminating unnecessary forms and reports should be followed. The key to success lies in one word—ruthlessness!

10. Adopting a Clear Desk policy

Everyone in the organization should be encouraged to work from a clear desk, not as an end in itself but as a means to helping them work more effectively to avoid the missed opportunities and deadlines, the distractions and the wasted time that characterize the cluttered desk.

Index

Archer, Jeffrey, 10

backlog, 20, 26-7, 40
Bain, Professor George, 11, 31, 39, 83, 127
Bethlehem Steel, 108
Body Shop, 43, 52, 151
Branson, Richard, 10, 52, 83, 103, 118
business letters, 3

Citibank Corporation, 1
Commission on Federal Paperwork, 64
computer printout, 4, 5
cost of paperwork, 6
crises, 30-2, 71-2

Davidson, Dr. Marilyn, 14
delegating, 97, 146, 153-4
desktop computers, 5
diaries, 155-6
distractions, 9, 30, 32-4, 125
Dupont, 130

Einstein, Albert, 13
electronic mail, 68-9

faxes, 5
filing,
    classification, 147-8
    priority, 136-7
    statistics, 130
    system, 18, 19, 90, 127-48

General Motors, 69
government paperwork, 6
Grand Metropolitan, 9, 52, 129

Harvey-Jones, Sir John, 9, 21, 45, 49, 52, 55, 88, 92, 95, 96, 99
hoarding, 133-4
H Samuel Group, 57

IBM, 70
indecision, 93
information,
 duplicated, 4, 55
 gap, 53
 technology, 5
 unnecessary, 80, 133
Inland Revenue, 4
interruptions, 40, 91, 115, 126

Lee, Ivy, 108, 109
London Business School, 11, 31
losing things, 35-7
Luin, Tsai, 3

mail, 18, 79
mailings, 81
Marks & Spencer, 58, 60, 61, 88, 134
Marks, Simon, 88
MCA, 87
McCormack, Mark, 82, 83
meetings, 16, 140
memos, 65-9, 75
Metcalfe, Admiral Joseph, 45
myths about paperwork, 11-6

Nordstrom, 70

open door policy, 75-6

paper fatigue, 30
paper handling skills, 5, 7, 103-26

paperholic boss, 76-9
paperless office, 5-6
paperwork diary, 99-101
Paperwork Reduction Act (U.S.), 64
Pareto principle, 117
Pareto, Vilfredo, 117
Perot, Ross, 69
personality, 13-4
personal organizers, 82, 137-8
photocopies, 5, 6, 133-4
planning, 18, 115
procedures, 70
productivity, 29-30
priorities, 118-123
private life, 27
procrastination, 38-40, 95, 126

Ratner, Gerald, 10, 26, 45, 57, 58, 65, 89,
97, 99, 118, 149
Rayner, Sir Derek, 59
reading, 16, 17, 141-2
recycled paper, 7
reports, 4,5, 38-9, 46, 54
Review of Administrative Forms in Government, 59
Roddick, Anita, 10, 43, 52
Rodgers, Buck, 70
Ryder Systems, 68

Schwab, Charles, 108, 109
Sheppard, Sir Allen, 9, 29, 35, 47, 52, 68, 85,
95, 96, 118, 129, 143
Sieff, Marcus, 58, 60, 62
staff morale, 4
standard forms, 4, 7, 55-65
stationery, 156
stress, 9, 40-1

telephone,
   conversations, 36
   messages, 23
time, 6
top-down approach, 124-5
Trump, Donald, 27

UMIST School of Management, 14
Virgin Airways, 52, 103, 118

Wasserman, Lew, 87
work patterns, 15

Zampino, Michael P., 1